2,50

Englis gregation

CW01636010

A Short History

by

Dom Bernard Green
Monk of Ampleforth

with a foreword by
Cardinal Basil Hume

CATHOLIC TRUTH SOCIETY
Publishers to the Holy See
38/40 ECCLESTON SQUARE
LONDON S

NIHIL OBSTAT: Dom Philip Jebb, Censor Deputatus

IMPRIMATUR: Victor Farwell, Abbas Praeses

Printed by The Lincoln's Inn Press Ltd., Standard House,
Bonhill Street, London, EC2A 4DA.

ISBN 0 85183 297 0

CONTENTS

HISTORICAL LIST OF MODERN HOUSES IN THE ENGLISH BENEDICTINE CONGREGATION

Monks

1607 Downside Abbey (St Gregory's; Douai) Stratton on the Fosse, Bath, Somerset, BA3 4RH (51 monks)
1608 Ampleforth Abbey (St Lawrence's; Dieulouard) York, YO6 4EN (123 monks)
1615 Douai Abbey (St Edmund's; Paris, then Douai) Upper Woolhampton, Reading, Berkshire, RG7 5TH (52 monks)
1859 Belmont Abbey, Hereford, HR2 9RZ (57 monks)
1876 St Benedict's Abbey, Fort Augustus, Inverness-shire, Scotland, PH32 4DB (32 monks)
1882 Buckfast Abbey, Buckfastleigh, Devon, TQ11 0EE (49 monks)
1897 Ealing Abbey, Charlbury Grove, London, W5 2DY (21 monks)
1919 St Gregory's Abbey, Cory's Lane, Portsmouth, Rhode Island 02871, USA (26 monks)
1924 St Anselm's Abbey, 4501 South Dakota Ave. N.E., Washington DC, 20017, USA (32 monks)
1933 Worth Abbey, Crawley, West Sussex, RH10 4SB (33 monks)
1955 St Louis Priory, 500 South Mason Rd, St Louis, Missouri 63141 USA (13 monks)

Nuns

1623 Stanbrook Abbey (Our Lady of Consolation; Cambray) Callow End, Worcester, WR2 4TD (59 nuns)
1651 St Mary's Abbey (Our Lady of Good Hope; Paris) Colwich, Little Haywood, Stafford, ST18 0UE (23 nuns)
1868 Talacre Abbey, Gronant, Prestatyn, Clwyd, Wales, LL19 9TD (23 nuns)
1892 St Scholastica's Abbey, Holme Eden, Warwick Bridge, Carlisle, Cumbria, CA4 8RD (12 nuns)

The numbers in brackets show the size of the communities in January, 1979.

FOREWORD

A Benedictine monk at his profession makes vows of obedience, stability and conversion of life. Rooted in a tradition, belonging to one community, he finds God through the Rule of St Benedict and the example and needs of his brethren. The history of his community and congregation are therefore of central importance to him, helping him to understand the life he is called to follow.

The Benedictines played a prominent part in English history from the times of the Anglo-Saxon Church, and their influence did not die, though it has often been forgotten, with the dissolution of the monasteries. English Christianity learnt much from the Benedictine spirit, and the history of the English Benedictines is a link with the past that goes beyond the Reformation and even beyond the split between Eastern and Western Christendom. The vitality of the modern Benedictines is an inspiration to rediscover our roots and illuminate our future.

G. B. Hume

Basil Hume
Cardinal Archbishop of Westminster

CHAPTER ONE: ORIGINS

Reformation and Restoration

When, in just four years between 1536 and 1540, the agents of Henry VIII closed the one hundred and thirty-seven houses of English Black Monks and the thirty-one houses of foreign Benedictine Congregations in England, they ended a tradition that stretched back for nearly a thousand years. Since St Augustine had established his cathedral church at Canterbury in 597 and begun the conversion of the Saxon kingdom of Kent, Christianity in England had taken its inspiration and even its shape and leadership from the monasteries. Though rivalled from the thirteenth century by the rise of new orders, the Black Monks following the Rule of St Benedict were never wholly eclipsed and held their position as the senior, the largest and perhaps the most influential religious body in the English Church. Their monasteries were more than centres of religious life; they were among the richest landowners in the kingdom, and there were fifty abbots and cathedral priors in the House of Lords. They administered seven of the cathedrals as Cathedral Priories, a unique English institution, where the monks were the cathedral chapter and the dean of the cathedral was prior of the monastery. They were part of the fabric of English government and society. All this was swept away with surprising ease by Henry's ministers. Four abbots and a few other monks were executed; the rest made no resistance. The monks were dispersed, pensioned off or found positions in the new Church establishment. Their property passed to the Crown, and then into the hands of new secular landlords.

With the accession of Henry's Catholic daughter, Mary I, communion with Rome and the full observance of the medieval Church were restored. With her cousin and adviser,

Cardinal Reginald Pole, she sought to re-establish monastic life in England. In 1555, sixteen former Black Monks, dressed in their monastic habits and led by Dr John Feckenham who had become Dean of St Paul's, appeared at court and petitioned the Queen to restore their monasteries. She responded with alacrity, and decided to restore Westminster Abbey, the great royal monastery and shrine of Edward the Confessor. Thus on 21 November 1556, conventual life was begun there again, with Feckenham as abbot and sixteen monks from various houses as the nucleus of the community. Its numbers quickly grew to fifty, many of them ex-monks from other houses. Such a diverse collection could not re-create the monastic regime that had existed at Westminster fifteen years before, and they were influenced by the continental monastic reform, especially that of the Italian monasteries known as the Cassinese Congregation, over which Pole was Cardinal Protector. Feckenham was therefore elected abbot for only three years, rather than for life, in accordance with the Cassinese reform.

It was a bold venture and an important part of Mary's attempt to restore English Catholicism, but it lasted only three years. With Mary's death and the accession of her Protestant sister Elizabeth, the monastery was again threatened with dissolution. They were offered the possibility of continued existence if they would accept the new Church settlement, but they preferred to be dispossessed. They were dispersed, the buildings once more put into the hands of a secular dean and chapter, and Abbot Feckenham spent the last twenty-four years of his life in prison.

Elizabeth's reign saw the resurgence of Catholicism in the Counter-Reformation, and her attempt at religious compromise was increasingly threatened by militant, vigorous and well-organised opposition from both Catholics and Puritans. But the Catholics were divided. Though they were strengthened and encouraged by the influx of seminary priests in the 1570s and the Jesuits in the 1580s, they lacked the authoritative leadership that only a bishop could provide, and fell into disunity with controversies over theology, spirituality and politics. Not every English Catholic shared the outlook of the Jesuits, which seemed to be revolutionary on all of these issues. Many preferred the ways of the past and many preferred a more eirenical approach to religious disputes and political rivalries. But all were animated by hopes for a speedy Catholic restoration. Elizabeth's heir for the first half of her reign was a Catholic, Mary Queen of Scots, and for the second half it was Mary's son, James Stuart, who was thought to be well-disposed towards his mother's co-religionists. Conditions seemed ripe for the revival of that most venerable and most English of the old religious orders, the Benedictines.

The first Benedictine house to be founded in exile was a community of nuns established in Brussels in 1598 by Lady Mary Percy, daughter of the martyred Earl of Northumberland, Blessed Thomas Percy. The nuns led lives of austere simplicity, strict enclosure and contemplative prayer. Their community flourished. In the eighteen years that Lady Mary presided as abbess, she professed forty-three nuns. The community was strongly influenced by Jesuit directors, and some of the nuns, including the abbess, wanted to replace them with secular priests, whereas others wanted to found a convent based more firmly on Jesuit principles. These differences were to prove fruitful a generation later, when the Brussels convent contributed to the foundation of two new communities.

It was in the same atmosphere of controversy that the first Englishmen made their way to Benedictine cloisters in Italy and Spain. In 1588, apparently to escape the broils between the secular clergy and the Jesuits in the English College in Rome, a young priest called Robert Sayer entered the monastery at Monte Cassino, St Benedict's own monastery and the house from which the Cassinese Congregation took its name. Significantly, he was given the name Gregory, that of the first pope to have been a monk, author of the first life of St Benedict and the man who sent St Augustine to England. Sayer was followed in the next few years by half a dozen others, among them Fr Thomas Preston and Fr Anselm Beech. They took with them both their considerable intellectual gifts and their hopes of returning to England to fulfil the missionary oath they had taken in the seminary. They were concerned that the Benedictines should not go unrepresented in any Catholic restoration in England. Ten years later, a similar exodus began from the English College in Valladolid to enter the Benedictine monasteries in Spain. Six left in 1599. Among the first to be clothed as a monk was Blessed Mark Barkworth, a priest on his way to England, who was executed at Tyburn in 1601. Also among the first generation were St John Roberts and Fr Augustine Bradshaw. They too had reacted against Jesuit influence in the seminary, and they were anxious to return to serve the English mission. The Englishmen in the Spanish and Italian monasteries petitioned Rome to be allowed to return, and permission was given in 1601 to the Cassinese and 1602 to the Spanish. It was especially remarkable that monks in the Spanish Congregation should obtain such permission as they were bound by a special vow of enclosure, but they were the first to land in England in 1602. This encouraged others to follow them into Spanish monasteries; in 1603, fifteen men left the English College in Valladolid for this purpose, and twenty-five more in the next three years. Bradshaw was made vicar-general for the English members of the Spanish Congregation in 1602, and soon saw the need for separate houses for his men. In 1606, he took lodgings in Douai, a university town in the Spanish Netherlands much patronised by the English Catholic refugees, and was given property in Lorraine by the Bishop of Verdun that had formerly been the church and monastery of a college of canons. Conventual life was begun at Douai under the patronage of St Gregory the Great in 1607, and in the following year in the abandoned buildings dedicated to St Lawrence at Dieulouard. More novices were attracted, among them a distinguished English exile, the Rector of the University at Rheims, Dr William Gifford. He was clothed at Rheims at the Abbey of St Remi for St Lawrence's with the name Gabriel in 1608. By 1610, he had become the second prior at Dieulouard, and in 1611 went to become the first prior of a new foundation at St Malo dedicated to St Benedict. In that year, Philippe de Caverel, Abbot of St Vedast in Arras, opened a college for his monks at Douai including a residence for the English monks who would teach there, and in 1612 the Abbot of Marchiennes also secured the services of the English monks for his college. In 1615, the indefatigable Bradshaw made a fourth foundation in Paris, which came in time to be dedicated to St Edmund.

Further encouragement was given to this little group by their first martyrs. In 1608, one of the first novices at Douai was executed at Tyburn, Blessed George Gervase. Two years later, St John Roberts, one of the first Benedictine missioners in England, was arrested in his vestments at the end of Mass. At his trial, he declared himself a member of the same order as St Augustine. He was executed at Tyburn. In 1612, Blessed Maurus Scott, another monk of the Spanish Congregation who had become a member of St Gregory's, died at Tyburn; in 1616, Blessed Thomas Tunstall, a secular priest clothed in England, died at Norwich.

As numbers grew, it seemed essential to establish a union between the English members of the Spanish and Cassinese Congregations, but it was difficult to find an acceptable agreement. Both wanted to preserve their independence, but they also wanted to lay claim to the Benedictine inheritance that might soon be theirs. The Cassinese found a possible solution. From about 1600, Fr Anselm Beech knew of the survival of one monk from Marian Westminster, Fr Sigebert Buckley. It seemed possible that Buckley could pass on the rights and privileges that the Westminster community had derived from the medieval English Congregation, but it was a complex and difficult matter. Beech was fortunate to be able to call on the services of a young monk of the Cassinese Congregation with considerable legal experience who was then working in London, a Welshman and lawyer by trade who had been Recorder of Abergavenny but who had had to interrupt his studies for the priesthood through ill-health, Br Augustine Baker. Baker carefully unravelled the complicated canonical questions, and determined the course of action to be followed. On 21 November 1607, the fifty-first anniversary of Westminster's refoundation, Buckley witnessed the profession of Robert Sadler and Edward Maihew as monks of the Cassinese Congregation and then affiliated them into Westminster, bestowing on them all the rights and privileges that he had inherited.

Thus a third group was added to the Cassinese and Spanish, the revived English Benedictine Congregation (EBC). It quickly grew in size as several more Cassinese were affiliated, Baker himself being the third. The Spanish welcomed this development, and in 1613 gave equal rights to the EBC at

Dieulouard, Maihew becoming prior the following year. But schemes for the union of the three groups failed. The principal figures were now Anselm Beech and Thomas Preston for the Cassinese, and Leander Jones and Rudesind Barlow for the Spanish. At last, after complicated negotiations, a union was drawn up in 1619 between the monks of the English and Spanish Congregations, recognised by the Papal brief *Ex Incumbenti*, by which both groups were amalgamated in the one re-established EBC but with the Spanish General as their ultimate superior. The Cassinese would not accept this, and remained independent to the end. Thus in 1619, with papal recognition, the EBC was restored with the Constitutions that were to shape its future for nearly three hundred years.

The Nature and Constitutions of the EBC

The Congregation reconstituted in 1619, though linked to the medieval one by juridical and sentimental ties, found its roots in the Spanish and Cassinese reform rather than the English past. The medieval English Congregation was a federation of autonomous houses, the abbots meeting on a regional basis for mutual encouragement and support. The continental congregations that were formed in the fifteenth century were far stronger bodies, less a group of individual abbeys than an order with a large number of separate but similar houses. They had come together for mutual protection from the encroachments of abbots appointed *in commendam*, who were given the titles and revenues of the abbot, but were seldom monks and sometimes not even clerics, and accepted none of the duties of the position. To save themselves from degenerating into royal sinecures, monasteries on the continent established a centralised system of government, a common observance and a vigorous independence of action. The fifteenth century was the age of the conciliar movement, when reformers recommended regular government of the Church by Ecumenical Councils. These two congregations reflected this outlook. They did not emphasise abbatial authority or the autonomy of the houses, but rather established rule by councils of senior monks, General Chapters, which met at regular intervals and appointed the officials in the separate houses and drew up the rules, or constitutions, that they would all follow: Their monastic spirituality was one of silence, solitude, personal austerity and above all mental prayer. This was all inherited by the EBC, and remained the distinctive hallmark of its spirituality, one that suited so well the needs of a mixed body, both missionary and conventual.

The EBC was exceptional in combining two separate systems of monastic government, the missioners in England under their provincials and the conventuals in the monasteries under their priors, all under the overall authority of the President and ultimately under the General Chapter that met every four years. All monks remained members of their own communities, but when they passed on to the mission they were taken from the authority of their prior and put under the authority of provincials, and followed quite different laws regarding property, dress and of course religious observance.

The monasteries were not unlike any of the severe, reformed houses of seventeenth-century Europe. They had a full regular life, with Matins at midnight or three a.m., the Office being sung slowly as 'real prayer', and Conventual Mass sung with full plainchant if there were four or more present. Mental prayer was prescribed for one half hour and two quarter hours daily. There was total abstinence from meat and frequent fasts. Though this rule was soon abandoned in most of the houses, it was replaced with a complete ban on smoking, the latest vice. Enclosure and silence were strictly observed, and there was strong emphasis on the importance of reading and study. It was not without its consolations: 'where games of chance are played, the stakes are to be brief prayers.'

St Gregory's in the university town of Douai was the largest of the three houses in the French-speaking territories, with a resident community usually between twenty-five and thirty strong in the seventeenth century, and between fifteen and twenty in the eighteenth. They had a small school, and often had juniors from other houses studying with them, while their theology professors lectured in the colleges of St Vedast and Marchiennes, part of the university. By contrast, St Lawrence's was smaller, poorer and far more remote in a small village in Lorraine, but its numbers stayed even at between 14 and 16 monks for two hundred years. They earned their living from a brewery, at times a source of some embarrassment. Despite its size, the community was influential beyond its numbers. Of the twenty-six presidents who ruled the EBC between 1619 and 1793, twelve were Lawrentians. The house was famous for its strict observance. St Edmund's in Paris set another contrast. It was in the heart of a fashionable world of Catholic exiles. Its numbers fluctuated more widely, sometimes larger than St Gregory's and sometimes smaller than St Lawrence's, and it was strongly influenced by the university and intellectual life in Paris. In the late seventeenth and early eighteenth centuries, it became a centre for Jacobite exiles, and James II and his Queen and their daughter Marie Louise were buried in the church.

A substantial proportion of these communities, perhaps between a half and a third, were juniors studying philosophy and theology in preparation for ordination. After a year's noviciate, a young man took solemn vows for life and then devoted a further six years to studying before he became a priest. He then spent at least a few more years in his monastery before being sent on the mission to England, the ultimate destination of most, though some remained in their monasteries all their lives. For the most part, they were communities of young men, ruled by priors appointed every four years by the General Chapter.

Along with the traditional monastic vows of stability, obedience and conversion of life, a novice took the missionary oath, pledging himself to return to England to serve on the mission at the bidding of the President. From the 1630s onwards, there were usually more monks working on the mission than resident in the monasteries. In England, they were placed under the authority of either the provincial of Canterbury in the south, or the provincial of York in the north. The provincials, each assisted by two definitors and a procurator, were also appointed by the General Chapter every four years and exercised the same power as priors. They were independent of each other, with separate funds, and only the President could transfer a monk from his monastery to the mission, or from one province to the other, or back to his monastery from the mission. In England, the missioners were expected to be self-sufficient and had to have private property called *peculium*; to be clothed as a novice, a man had to have an income of £12 p.a. or a fortune of £300, or some recognised qualifications that guaranteed his livelihood. As the missions became more stable in the eighteenth century, it became common for monks to sink their *peculium* into the mission or into the province, and live off an allowance; many of them became great benefactors of their brethren and their people. In England, they were unable to wear the habit, and even when returning to the Continent for a brief visit to their monastery tended not to wear monastic dress, as it became identified as the sign of being a conventual, with different status and obligations, nor were they obliged to attend choir office. Attempts were made to ensure that the missioners kept in touch with their communities, as for example in insisting on regular retreats made by them in their monasteries, but it was not easy to comply with such regulations. Discipline and religious life on the mission was maintained by friendly mutual support, and the priests met often in their provinces or at a county level, and also by the supervision of the provincials, but for the most part it was an isolated, almost eremitical life, and most missioners spent their days in quiet, remote rural missions.

Of course, these two separate structures of monastic government and styles of life could not exist in parallel without some friction. From the first, there were difficulties between the conventuals who wanted a stricter monastic observance and the missioners who wanted to work unhindered at the conversion of England. A leading protagonist in the early period was Fr Rudesind Barlow, who was unsparing in his endeavours to make the missioners more overtly monastic. But even he had to respect the heroism and the success of the men who risked their lives in England: his own brother was a martyr, St Ambrose Barlow.

The General Chapter presided over both monasteries and missions. It met every four years and consisted of congregational officials, such as a Procurator in Curia who represented the EBC in Rome, a secretary to the Chapter, a secretary to the President, and a Master of Studies, together with the superiors on the mission and in the houses, the provincials and priors and the President and his definitors, and twelve holders of honorary positions known as Cathedral Priorships, titular dignities in memory of the monastic medieval cathedrals. As the Chapter itself appointed all these officials and bestowed the titular honours, it was a self-perpetuating oligarchy, for the most part consisting of old men not exercising direct jurisdiction. It was therefore a conservative body, but around its quadrennial meetings the history of the EBC revolved.

The President was responsible to the Chapter, and was in effect its chief executive. The authority of the Spanish General was soon repudiated, and the President had supreme power in the Congregation between meetings of the Chapter, and individual monks took their vows to him. Yet even he had a check imposed upon him, with two definitors who acted as a court of appeal against his decisions, and the Chapter every four years reviewed his administration and either re-appointed him or chose another President. This style of government gave the EBC stability and sufficient sharing of power to preserve it for three hundred years.

Early Development

The restored EBC took its complexion and character from the reformed monasticism of Italy and Spain, and also, increasingly as the seventeenth century passed, from the movements of French monasticism. Among these great Benedictine congregations, the English monks acquired a reputation for learning and rigorous observance that they first found in Italy. Both Gregory Sayer and Thomas Preston taught theology at Monte Cassino, and other early members of the Cassinese Congregation such as Edward Maihew, Anselm Beech and Augustine Baker were notable scholars. They attracted learned men into their ranks, such as Gabriel Gifford who had been Rector of the University of Rheims, and ten years after becoming a Benedictine was chosen as co-adjutor bishop of Rheims, as assistant to the Archbishop whom he succeeded in 1622, becoming first Peer of France. Abbot de Caverel first endowed the house at Douai to be a house of studies where his own monastery might find good theology lecturers. Fr Rudesind Barlow, the second President of the EBC and twice prior of St Gregory's, was professor of theology in the college of St Vedast in Douai for forty years, and Fr Leander Jones, who alternated with him as president and prior, was Regius Professor of Hebrew at Douai for 24 years. It was the need for good theology teachers that impelled the German Bursfeld Congregation during the Thirty Years' War to grant the EBC a house in Germany. With two of their monasteries in university cities, it was a reputation that the English monks never lost, though later generations seldom matched the stature of their founders.

To some extent, they were impelled in their researches into monastic history and ascetical and dogmatic theology by the need to clarify and deepen their understanding of their own position in English Catholicism. In the 1620s a major work of historical scholarship by Edward Maihew, the *Trophaea Benedictinorum*, which was intended to establish the claims of the EBC to inherit the medieval English monastic tradition, was challenged by two English monks, Fr Francis Walgrave and Fr John Barnes. Barnes put forward the argument that the medieval English Congregation had really been the Cluniac French Congregation, which therefore inherited all the old rights and privileges. Walgrave transferred his allegiance to Cluny, and turned the house where he lived as chaplain to the great French convent of Chelles into an English Cluniac priory and began to take novices. This argument undermined the claims of the EBC and questioned its validity, and in response Fr Clement Reyner, with the assistance of Augustine Baker, produced a massive historical vindication of their position, the *Apostolatus Benedictinorum in Anglia*. Walgrave at last gave way, but poor Barnes fell into the hands of the Roman Inquisition where he was accused of heterodox opinions about relations with the Anglican Church, and was at last declared insane and confined to an asylum for the rest of his life. The EBC's position was thereafter ratified in the strongest terms in the papal bull *Plantata* of 1633.

The English Benedictines were always an amalgam of contemplative and active elements; the first impetus back towards Benedictine life had been from women seeking strict enclosure and regular observance, and now the EBC received a second infusion of contemplative spirit from the nuns. Fr Rudesind Barlow asked the Brussels community to spare three of their sisters to help found a new convent at Cambray which would be directly part of the EBC. The venture began in 1623, and in 1625 the first generation of nine nuns was professed, three of them cousins with the surname More, great-great-granddaughters of St Thomas. Almost from the first, the community passed under the spiritual direction of Fr Augustine Baker, who developed his teaching on prayer and the spiritual life to meet their needs. Under the energetic leadership of Abbess Catherine Gascoigne and Dame Gertrude More, the little community turned away from the Jesuit forms of prayer followed at Brussels, and discovered in Baker a tradition of mystical prayer more suited to their temperament and needs. It was not a transition made without difficulty, but the nuns at Cambray became learned and experienced defenders of what was more an attitude than a system, and through them the writings of the fourteenth-century English mystics were preserved for later generations.

In the year after the foundation at Cambray, the Brussels nuns opened a very different house at Ghent. Its foundress was Dame Lucy Knatchbull, a woman of inspiring vision and tireless ability, who led a small group away from Brussels, which was overburdened with growing numbers, and created at Ghent a community that followed Jesuit principles closely. Vocations soon made it necessary at both Cambray and Ghent to make further foundations: at Paris from Cambray in 1651, and from Ghent at Dunkirk in 1662 and at Ypres in 1665. All of these convents remained independent of the EBC except Cambray, though the Paris nuns were regularly supplied with EBC chaplains.

The rapid expansion of the houses of nuns was equalled by the development of the houses of men. As the forces of the Counter-Reformation pushed back the Protestants in Germany during the Thirty Years' War, the German Bursfeld Congregation welcomed requests from the EBC for the use of German monasteries recovered from Protestant territory. Valuing the English monks' reputation for learning, they also saw them as potential evangelisers of the Lutheran countryside. Several deserted monasteries were promised to the EBC, but Lamspring, a former nunnery, was the only one they came permanently to inhabit, with Clement Reyner taking up residence in 1644 as the first abbot. Among the EBC houses, it was an anomaly. It alone had life-abbots, a stipulation in the Bursfeld gift. It ran a small school, but was well-endowed, and was richer, larger, more self-sufficient and more magnificent than the other monasteries. A succession of great abbots from gentry and aristocratic families, ruling for long periods, built there splendidly and well, but also extravagantly, to compete with the great German Baroque monasteries. It had the largest Baroque church in north Germany.

These little communities, though influenced by the currents of monastic reform around them, remained obstinately English. A few native laybrothers were admitted to some of them, but almost all the priests were Englishmen, looking forward to the day when their monasteries could be restored on English soil. At St Malo, this proved an area of dispute. When a laybrother called Anselm Prodhomme left the monastery and had himself ordained, it strengthened the demands of a party within the monastery that wanted the house to become wholly French and part of the Maurist Congregation. After prolonged and furious disputes, St Malo was sold to the Maurists in 1668. It was taken as a lesson by the others.

Fr Augustine Baker

The EBC derived its spiritual outlook as well as its practical organisation and intellectual standing from the example and inspiration of the Cassinese and Spanish Congregations. They belonged to a fifteenth-century reform, with a great emphasis on private prayer, spiritual reading and silence. But the EBC also inherited the tradition of the fourteenth-century English mystics, and preserved their teaching on prayer and the spiritual life for posterity. The greatest English spiritual writer since the Reformation, the man who rediscovered the English mystics and blended their teaching with that of the sixteenth- and seventeenth-century French and Spanish writers and the fourteenth-century Rhineland mystics, was a Benedictine, Augustine Baker.

David Baker was a Welshman, the son of the steward of Lord Abergavenny, and was brought up to speak fluently both Welsh and English. Born in 1575, he was at school in London at

Christ's Hospital during the attempted invasion by the Armada, which earned him two months' holiday. He then went on to Oxford, where his studies did not progress, and his father sent him instead to study Law at the Inner Temple, and as a lawyer he flourished. At about the age of twenty-five, after the death of his elder brother who had been studying with him in London, he returned home to Wales, but almost met his own death crossing a dangerous river. The experience precipitated a religious conversion, followed in 1603 by his conversion to Catholicism. He was advised to return to London and seek out the company and guidance of Catholic religious, and it was there that he met Anselm Beech and Thomas Preston. They encouraged him to try his vocation as a monk in Italy, and in 1605 he was clothed as a novice at the monastery of Santa Giustina in Padua, significantly with the name Augustine, the apostle of England. Ill-health forced an untimely return to England, but he continued his noviciate studies in London and gave himself wholeheartedly to the practice of private prayer that he had learnt in Padua. This first enthusiasm gradually faded, but he worked and studied in England for eighteen years, using his legal expertise to determine the proper course to preserve the continuity with the medieval Congregation through Fr Sigebert Buckley, and himself being the third to be incorporated into the EBC. When in 1619 the new Constitutions established the EBC and missioners had to become members of one of the provinces, and men already affiliated into the EBC from the Italian Congregation had to choose a monastery to which to belong, Baker was the first priest to put himself under the authority of the first Provincial of Canterbury, Robert Sadler, and along with most of the ex-Cassinese selected Dieulouard as his monastery, though he never lived there.

1619 also saw a new conversion, a return in Baker's life to the ways of prayer and personal austerity. He prayed for long hours each day, and devoted the rest of his time to research on material for Reyner's great *Apostolatus*, working alongside two of the great scholars of the age, Seldon and Cotton. In 1624, the work for Reyner completed, he was sent to Cambray to become the spiritual director of the community. It was a congenial appointment. In his conferences to the nuns, he developed his ideas about the spiritual life, and he read widely in mystical literature, much of which he translated for their use. They were nine years of enormous productivity, and a tradition of what came to dubbed 'Bakerism' was established among his disciples within the community.

The main lines of his theories were already clear. Reacting against the emphasis on formal methods of meditation so common in his own time, he stressed that real prayer was not so much thinking about God as an imageless, quiet craving for Him. Prayer was not a work of the mind or the emotions, but was more simple, more passive. When a soul found that it was no longer satisfied with thoughts about God but needed to pray to Him directly, he advocated the use of forced acts, little phrases repeated slowly in a set pattern, that could still and focus the attention in prayer. These would gradually be needed less as the soul found more ease in prayer through practice and perseverance, and at length the soul would find a prayer of aspirations, the direct work of the Holy Spirit giving a spirit of prayer at all times. Perhaps Baker's greatest strength was the way he linked this path with the externals of religious life. Mortification was the other and indispensable side of the quest for God, but by that he meant nothing extraordinary or rigorous, but rather a growing acceptance of God's will, in sickness and inconveniences, in reversals and irksome duties as well as in the joys and contentment of life. He made some incisive attacks on contemporary trends, such as the reliance on spiritual directors, formal meditation, a multiplicity of devotional or ascetical practices, a scrupulosity that derived from a preoccupation with one's own sins. He advocated far more freedom, personal discretion and openness than was then common, and it made him the delight of the nuns and the most controversial spiritual writer of the age.

His position as spiritual guide but not chaplain at Cambray led to increasingly difficult relations with the chaplain, and finally to his removal to the monastery at Douai. There he led a very retired life from 1633 until 1638, not attending the choir office and frequented by large numbers of people seeking advice about the spiritual life. He became a cause of dispute in the community between Bakerists and non-Bakerists. The most eminent man at Douai was Fr Rudesind Barlow, who had once been among Baker's warmest supporters, using his writings in the training of novices. Baker was not pleased when Barlow used one of his treatises, an account of the EBC's English mission, as ammunition in his attempt to force more monastic practices on the missioners. Baker wrote a preface for his treatise in which he lampooned the polypragmatic, ever-busy, quite unspiritual conventual, clearly a direct attack on Barlow to whom he handed the manuscript personally. Of course, his days at Douai were finished. He was sent, despite his age and infirmity, on the English mission. Accepting the decision humbly, he travelled over to an England fast approaching political crisis in 1638. For three years he lived prayerfully, but only one step ahead of the pursuivants, and then died in 1641 of an undiagnosed illness, shortly before the opening of the Civil War and the new purge of Catholic priests that claimed many victims.

His memory and his writings were treasured at Cambray, and a young generation of Bakerists grew up who wrote a series of biographies of him and popularised his teaching. He wrote in a flaccid and tortuous style, but he had all the assurance of a master. He also had the good fortune to be followed by a disciple of real insight and great learning, and considerably more literary ability, who could edit and amalgamate his prolific treatises into one of the most satisfactory handbooks of the spiritual life: *Sancta Sophia*, compiled in 1657 by Fr Serenus Cressy.

Hopes for a Catholic Restoration

Each Stuart monarch in turn took a Catholic bride. The Catholic states in Europe, Spain, France and Italy, were the most advanced politically and culturally. Increasingly in the seventeenth century, England looked to their example for its inspiration. Catholicism seemed fashionable, modern and intellectually compelling, and hopes for a Catholic restoration ran high. While the Jesuits were the object of widespread suspicion, thought to have extreme political views and to condone treason and assassination, the Benedictines were a traditionally royalist order. They therefore looked to the court for patronage, and some monks were present at the court of Charles I. Fr Leander Jones was buried in the Chapel Royal of Somerset House in 1635.

But Stuart indulgence of the Catholics did not pass uncriticised. It was one of the grievances among pious Protestants that led to the Civil War. The purge of Catholic priests that began in 1641 was the result of the pressure of the Long Parliament on Charles I, and it claimed the first victims of his reign apart from two executed at Lancaster in 1628. This persecution, and the war that led to the death of the King, deepened Benedictine loyalty to the Stuart family. An edict was passed in 1640, ordering all Jesuits and seminary priests to leave the country on penalty of death, and widespread arrests followed. Several Benedictines died in prison during the war. In Newgate, Fr Lawrence Mabbs in 1641, Fr Placid Peyto in 1643 and Fr Boniface Wilford in 1646; and in the Clink, Fr Benedict Cox in 1648. Three priests were harrassed to death in Yorkshire by Parliamentary troops on 26 July 1646: Fr Ildephonsus Hanson, Fr Boniface Kemp and Fr William Middleton. But the greatest figures in this persecution were St Ambrose Barlow, St Alban Roe and Blessed Philip Powel.

Ambrose Barlow was the brother of Rudesind, and like him a monk of St Gregory's. He had worked in his native Lancashire for 24 years before he was seized by a mob on Easter Sunday, 1641, and carried off to the magistrate. As news reached Fr Rudesind at Douay of his brother's arrest, he was taking part in the meeting of General Chapter. At once he resigned his Cathedral Priorship, and Fr Ambrose was elected in his place, but the execution took place before he could be told. He was hanged, drawn and quartered at Lancaster on September 10. Alban Roe was a monk of St Lawrence's who had worked in England for many years, but spent the last seventeen in the Fleet Prison. His confinement was not strict, and he did much apostolic work both in the prison and in the City of London. He was transferred to Newgate, tried and then executed at Tyburn in January 1642. His unfailing sense of humour shocked the dour ministers sent to try and convert him, but encouraged his fellow Catholics. Philip Powel was a Welshman who had been educated at the expense of Fr Augustine Baker, with whom he later studied Law in London. He became a monk at Douai, and after his ordination, worked once more for a time with Baker in London. He worked on the mission for twenty-four years before he was arrested and brought to trial in 1646. In court, he revealed all his skill as a lawyer, arguing every point of the case, claiming that in the Civil War the statute could not be applied, but when all his objections were ignored and he was condemned to death, he simply said, 'Deo Gratias'. On the scaffold, he declared himself a monk of the same order as Gregory the Great and Augustine.

After the war, the Stuart court in exile was attended by several Benedictines, among them Fr John Huddlestone, who had saved Charles II's life after the Battle of Worcester. At the Restoration, Huddlestone was one of the chaplains set up at Somerset House. Another was Serenus Cressy, formerly a Fellow of Merton and Dean of Leighlen in Ireland, and chaplain as an Anglican to several members of the nobility. He was part of the fashionable set that had gone over to Rome in the 1640s, and became a monk at Douai. When he had to return to the Continent later, he devoted his energies to scholarly labours in preserving the fourteenth-century English mystics and the works of Augustine Baker. Charles's brother was a Catholic, and his retinue also contained Benedictine chaplains. Catholic fortunes had not seemed so promising for a century.

In 1666 the General Chapter was held for the first time in London, and in 1669 another was actually held in St James's Palace. But Charles was still less secure than he seemed, and had to bend to pressure. In 1675 he was forced to dismiss his wife's chaplains from the court. Huddlestone was expressly excluded from the statute, and two laybrothers also remained, not included in the terms of the act. Three years later, the two laybrothers fell victim to the Titus Oates plot, and though Br Austin Rumley was acquitted, Blessed Thomas Pickering was found guilty and suffered at Tyburn in 1679. Huddlestone remained, and was therefore available in 1685 when Charles was on his deathbed, refusing the ministrations of an Anglican bishop, and at his brother's suggestion calling for a priest.

James was a far less supple character than his brother. At once, he reinstated the monks at court, inviting them to open a monastery in his palace at St James's. The monks wore the habit publicly on the King's instructions. In 1685 the General Chapter was held in the palace, but the Fathers were careful to make it plain that they would not welcome the royal presence at their deliberations. When James increased the number of

Catholic bishops, the vicars apostolic, in England from one to four, he put the poorest and least Catholic of the four districts, the Western District, into the hands of one of his Benedictine chaplains, Fr Philip Ellis. Bishop Ellis was consecrated in the Chapel Royal at St James's Palace in 1688, the first English Benedictine bishop since the Reformation, and the first of a succession of regulars, most of them Benedictines, to preside over the Western District.

When James fell in 1688 he took the English Benedictines with him into exile. Bishop Ellis attended him at the court of St Germains. Charles's widow, Queen Catherine of Braganza, lived on at Somerset House, still served by Fr John Huddlestone, who remained even after she left England in 1692, dying at Somerset House in 1698. There was no purge of the Catholic clergy comparable to those that had previously accompanied attacks on the Stuarts, and the missioners were little affected. On the Continent it still seemed that James had suffered only a temporary reverse, and he still had French support. The English monks showed continued loyalty to him and his family. James made his retreats at St Edmund's, and was at length buried there. A monk of St Edmund's, Br Bennet Weldon, compiler of an invaluable set of annals of EBC history, wrote a life of him. Strong Jacobite sympathies only gradually subsided, as the English government proved its strength against France in the War of the Spanish Succession and against the Jacobite rebels in the rising of 1715. Sheer realism forced the EBC to abandon its Jacobite hopes, and with them all hope of a rapid monastic restoration. Instead they faced a long, apparently endless task of maintaining the English mission. It demanded a reappraisal of their attitudes and their life, and it precipitated the most severe crisis they ever experienced.

Crisis and Realignment

The collapse of Jacobite hopes was followed by a period of unrest and disaffection, especially at the house most open to Jacobite influences, St Edmund's in Paris. Fr Bede Moore became the centre of a dissident party, who proved intractable to their superiors and gave great scandal. After ten years of notoriety, Moore joined a monk of St Gregory's working in

England, Fr Lawrence Fenwick, in his ambitious design to become President of the EBC, which they accomplished in 1717 with Moore as first Definitor. It quickly became apparent that the Congregation had fallen into the hands of a faction, and that the normal procedures for controlling the decisions and deeds of the President were unworkable. When Fenwick and Moore decided to reverse a decision of the 1717 Chapter and hold the next General Chapter in London and not at Douai, their opponents chose to make a stand. Several senior monks, including more than one ex-president, supported an appeal to Rome to uphold the 1717 decision. Rome granted the appeal, but Fenwick and Moore ignored it. Thus in 1721 two Chapters met, one in London and one at Douai, and each elected its own President. The schism ended when Fenwick and Moore's party melted away, leaving them obdurate and isolated, preferring a miserable vagrant existence in England for the rest of their lives, even spending years in debtors' prisons, to reconciliation. The Chapter Fathers showed great concern for their welfare, subsidising them and paying their debts; they took the money but refused to return.

Despite this schism, the EBC passed into the second quarter of the eighteenth century united, but with a far less well-defined sense of purpose. The nuns still devoted themselves to prayer for the conversion of England, but it seemed an ever more distant reality. Support from the gentry and nobility slackened, and by the middle of the century power in the Congregation had passed from men from families such as the Howards, Tempests, Fenwicks, Riddells and Southcotes, into the hands of men from Lancashire farming or middle-class families, the Naylors, Brewers, Heatleys, Sharrocks and Marshes. It was a transition that reflected the transformation of the English Catholic body, with the disappearance of recusant gentry families through death and apostasy, and the emergence of a new and vigorous Catholic middle class. As the leadership was taken by these men, it shifted from one group of families, with their close network of inter-relationships, their shared values and political outlook, to another that was similarly united by marriage and kinship, and by the different but equally strong assumptions and aspirations of their Lancashire background. They were a group that was to dominate the EBC for a hundred and fifty years, to lead it through the years of expansion and development in the nineteenth century and into the twentieth.

In keeping with this transition, new parishes were developed to supplement or replace the gentry chaplaincies that had been the backbone of the Benedictine mission. As the gentry died out or embraced Anglicanism, new missions under the direct control of the priests, and not their patrons, replaced them. In 1766 the mission at Woolton was endowed by Lady Molyneux in the year before her death to preserve Catholicism in that part of Lancashire. In 1774 the Warwick Bridge mission replaced the chaplaincy at Warwick Hall in Cumberland. In 1780 the mission at Aberford in Yorkshire was developed to succeed the chaplaincy to the Gascoignes of Parlington who had conformed. In 1793 Ampleforth replaced the chaplaincy at Gilling Castle when the last Catholic Fairfax died. These added to the missions that were already independent, growing in size and building new churches, or being moved to follow the drift in population. For example, the first church was opened at Brindle in 1735, more than fifty years after the establishment of the mission, and was replaced by another in 1787. In 1771 the first parish was founded in Warrington from Woolston, two miles away. Brownedge was founded from Cuerdon in 1780.

But the EBC was following developments in the Catholic body rather than anticipating or initiating them. They did not seize opportunities of moving into the larger towns, and were content for most of the century with two urban missions, London and Bath, the former overshadowed by the many missions in the city and the latter to some extent a showcase for aristocratic visitors to the spa. An important factor in this lack of coherence and overall vision in the organisation of the missions was the weakness of the provincial structure. Missions had, for the most part, to be self-sufficient. It therefore fell to rich patrons, large congregations, or generous missioners to make real changes in the parishes, and provincials tended to be cautious about undertaking new responsibilities or serious financial burdens. Coventry and Liverpool were accepted reluctantly from the Franciscans and Jesuits, the pioneering work completed, and only a man of remarkable energy and pastoral zeal such as Fr Bennet

Macdonald could overcome the hesitations and doubts of his provincial and develop a new urban mission. Having inherited and resolved bitter disputes in the Jesuit parish of St Mary's, he opened a second Liverpool mission at Seel Street in 1788. He was a prolific writer, with strong pastoral instincts, composing an English book of prayers for use in church, the *Companion to the Altar*; but several of his early curates proved unequal to the demands of the apostolate to the oppressed poor of a fast-developing port, and they were sent back to their monasteries suffering from scruples.

Despite the caution, the missions were increasingly seen as the senior part of the EBC's work. Congregational officials were increasingly to be found living on the mission, and it became difficult to find men prepared to undertake the task of ruling the monasteries as priors, while the growth in independent missions made the role of the provincials more important. Yet the houses in France did not lose their character as intellectual centres. Influenced by the French enlightenment through the universities at Douai and Paris, the theology teaching came to emphasise the scientific developments of the age, and questions such as the relationship between faith and reason, or revelation and natural religion. The approach to study was historical and critical. In the course of studies drawn up in 1764 for EBC theology students, wide reading in non-Catholic and Jansenistic authors was prescribed in contemporary theological and philosophical literature, as well as a broad sweep of Catholic writing modelled on Mabillon's *Traité des Etudes Monastiques*. A good example of the intellectual attainment of the English monks in this period was Fr Bede Brewer, sent from Dieulouard to study at the Sorbonne in the 1760s and 1770s under an English expatriate and controversial theologian, the Abbé Luke Joseph Hooke, finally obtaining the Doctorate of Divinity with highest distinction for producing a new edition of Hooke's book on natural religion. Hooke had other English Benedictine pupils than Brewer, and his own sister was a nun, and finally abbess, at Cambray.

Perhaps the most prominent English monk of the second half of the eighteenth century was Fr Charles Walmesley, a Lancashireman professed at St Edmund's in 1739 when barely seventeen years of age. He early devoted himself to the study of mathematics and theology, earning a doctorate of Divinity from the Sorbonne for his theological studies and membership of the Royal Society of Berlin and a Fellowship of the Royal Society in London for his mathematical works. He was only twenty-seven years old when he was elected Prior of St Edmund's in 1749, but he had already acquired an international reputation as a mathematician. In 1752, he was consulted by the British government on the revision of the calendar. Two years later, he became Procurator in Curia for the EBC and while in Rome was selected by Bishop York, the Benedictine Vicar Apostolic of the Western District, as his co-adjutor. He was consecrated in 1756, and took up residence at Bath where he lived at the Benedictine mission for thirty years. From 1764, on the retirement of Bishop York, he ruled the vicariate alone until 1781, when he selected Fr Gregory Sharrock, the Prior of St Gregory's, as his co-adjutor.

Walmesley gradually left his mathematical work behind him. His most creative years had been in his twenties and early thirties, but age and the demands of office forced him to narrow his interests. His theological work became increasingly eccentric; he devoted long hours to puzzling out the mathematical conundrums in the Apocalypse, issuing in pessimistic conclusions about the future. In 1780, a riot in Bath demolished the mission and his papers were burnt; his pessimism seemed confirmed. At about this time, he abandoned his mathematical studies altogether, after finding himself tracing diagrams on the corporal with the paten at Mass. As the most senior bishop in England, it fell to him to lead the recusants into the new freedom offered by the Relief Acts of 1778 and 1791, but he adopted an authoritarian and conservative attitude towards the gentry who formed the Catholic Committee pressing for further relief, possibly in doing so compromising the Catholic position in the assurances they were prepared to offer the Government. The characteristic Protestant fear of English Catholicism was threefold: an aversion to superstition, a fear of foreign or domestic tyranny whether from Spain or France or the Stuarts, and a suspicion of papal claims interfering with national autonomy. The Catholic Committee sought to allay those fears by presenting an English Catholicism that was Cisalpine or

Gallican, not papalist, that was liberal and humane, that was democratic and enlightened. One English Benedictine, Fr Cuthbert Wilks, played a significant role in the work of the Catholic Committee, and earned thereby Bishop Walmesley's special disapprobation. He too was a monk of St Edmund's, trained at the Sorbonne, though he had not taken the doctorate in Divinity as he saw no need to bind himself with the oath affirming the Immaculate Conception, then a qualification for taking the degree. He impressed Dr Johnson on his visit to Paris in 1775, as related in Boswell. He belonged to a later generation than Walmesley, a generation for whom the enlightenment was philosophical and political as well as scientific. Once the French Revolution had discredited the rationalism and liberalism of Wilks and his friends, and gave added force to the pessimism and conservative reaction of Walmesley and the other bishops, Wilks had to move on to the defensive. At length he was obliged to leave England, and lived the last twenty-nine years of his life on the Continent, finally retiring to live with his own community and dying at Douai.

Walmesley's was the stern voice of old-fashioned English recusancy. He was, for example, the last Vicar Apostolic to insist that permission was needed in his district to eat meat in Lent. He died, after forty years as a bishop, in 1797. But the tradition of liberal and enlightened English Catholicism of men such as Wilks and Brewer did not disappear with the French Revolution or even later with the new ultramontanism of the second half of the nineteenth century. It was so natural a part of the Benedictine ethos as it had developed in England for two hundred years that it was one of the main forces colouring and shaping the EBC in the nineteenth and twentieth centuries.

CHAPTER TWO: THE RESETTLEMENT IN ENGLAND

The French Revolution and the Resettlement

By the 1780s the future of the houses on the Continent seemed precarious. As ever, Lamspring was an exception. The grand building schemes and financial mismanagement of Abbot Rokeby in the middle years of the century had incurred heavy debts, but his successor, Abbot Maurus Heatley, restored the monastery's fortunes to comfortable prosperity. But the other three houses of men were not so secure. The school at Douai was not flourishing; Prior Augustine Moore ruled for twenty years in the third quarter of the century, building extensively and expanding the school, but his successor, Prior Gregory Sharrock, allowed the school to decline in numbers and his brother Jerome Sharrock, who succeeded him when he became co-adjutor to Bishop Walmesley, filled the school with French boys. The finances at Dieulouard were not healthy. There were signs of disaffection among the young men at St Edmund's. Various plans were proposed to amalgamate the houses on the model of the Maurist Congregation; one suggestion had Douai still running the school, the noviciate at Lamspring, the juniorate at Paris with access to the Sorbonne, and Dieulouard as the house of preparation for junior priests about to go on the mission. In 1781 a common noviciate was opened at Douai, and a small school at Dieulouard to train boys for the noviciate, but the arrangements were unsuccessful and were abandoned in 1785. The monasteries drew the great majority of their vocations from Lancashire. In 1774, for example, St

Lawrence's was found to be entirely composed of Lancashiremen save a few French oblates and one postulant.

The communities were saved by the French Revolution. It forced them to make the move that was essential for their future, the return to England. The General Chapter was held in London in 1789, and two new priors were appointed, Fr Henry Parker at St Edmund's and Fr Richard Marsh at St Lawrence's, who was barely eligible at the age of twenty-seven years. Dame Christina Hooke, the sister of the Abbé Hooke who lectured at the Sorbonne, became Abbess of Cambray in the same year, but she died in 1792. The three priors, Jerome Sharrock, Marsh and Parker, reacted in much the same way to the events of the Revolution. At first, along with everybody else, they did not see the threat to their position; in 1790, when the new government dissolved the religious orders, they secured exemption for the English communities. Prudently, they dispensed themselves from wearing the habit in 1791, but life continued little changed until 1793, when the war with England transformed the situation. The French boys were sent home from the Douai school, and arrangements were made for part of each community to return to England, though the priors planned to remain with a few monks to guard their property. In Paris, Parker had no option, for along with the President, Augustine Walker, the first president to have lived in one of the monasteries for many years, he was held prisoner in his own house. In October, Sharrock and the monks at Douai were arrested and taken to Doullens, where they shared their imprisonment with the Jesuits from St Omers for nearly a year, keeping to the monastic regime as far as possible. At the same time, the community was arrested at Dieulouard, with the exception of three monks, including Prior Marsh who escaped and swam the Moselle and only discovered that the other two had also escaped when he crossed the border to Trier. One of them was a laybrother, Br William Sharrock, the younger brother of the bishop and Prior of St Gregory's. Marsh returned to England and joined the survivors from Douai at Acton Burnell, where Sir Edward Smythe had given the refugees hospitality in his own house. In 1794, Marsh became prior of the joint communities, a dubious privilege that he relinquished after a year, when Sharrock and the other

Gregorians were released and made their way to Acton Burnell.

The nuns at Paris, Cambray and Dunkirk were all imprisoned for a time, the Cambray community sharing their imprisonment with the Carmelites at Compiègne who were later guillotined. They did not obtain their freedom and cross the Channel until 1795. Already, with the approach of war, the nuns of Brussels and Ghent had returned to England, where they found many French priests and nuns seeking refuge from the Revolution, among them the Benedictine community of Montargis, who had come over in 1792 and were to settle permanently in England. The Irish Dames of Ypres survived on the Continent until they were forced to retire to Ireland by the war of 1914.

As the nuns reached England, they found themselves destitute, but not friendless. They showed magnificent courage and resource in making a new home for themselves and preserving their religious life, and were fortunate to find loyal supporters. One such was Dr Bede Brewer, the missioner at Woolton near Liverpool, who had been chaplain to the nuns at Paris while studying for his doctorate at the Sorbonne. He gave the Cambray nuns a home at the little school he had established at Woolton, overcoming their reluctance to undertake the school with his forceful personality and strong common sense. He met the Paris nuns as they disembarked, and helped them find a home at Marnhull in Dorset, where he proved a benefactor and protector. The Brussels nuns found their way to Winchester, where they found a loyal supporter in Bishop Milner. He also befriended the Ghent nuns when they settled at Caverswall Castle in Staffordshire. The nuns from Dunkirk were fortunate to be given the Mary Ward convent at Hammersmith. But for all of them, it was a time of great hardship, in which they showed characteristically quiet resignation and perseverance.

At Acton Burnell, for all the earlier schemes of bringing the houses together in closer union, the experiment of putting two communities under one roof did not prove a success, and neither St Gregory's nor St Lawrence's forgot the experience. Prior Marsh decided to move away, and chose the mission at Brindle in Lancashire as the most suitable home for his monks.

It had been an independent mission for more than a hundred years, and the missioner, Fr Lawrence Hadley, had built a new church and house. But Hadley was reluctant to move; he was a Gregorian, and had lived at Brindle for thirty years. When Marsh went to call on him, he was prevented from even reaching the house by the congregation gathered in the garden, protesting that they did not want to lose their priest. Instead, Marsh began a series of moves in 1795 that took him to Birkenhead, to Scoles, to Vernon Hall and then to Parbold, founding a school on the way but exhausting the dwindling community. At last, in 1802, Marsh himself resigned and was succeeded by Fr Anselm Appleton. Numbers had been reduced to three priests and the redoubtable Br William Sharrock, but already the new president, the energetic and superbly able Bede Brewer, had begun negotiations for a further move. He had tried Brindle, and he now turned his attention across the Pennines to the house owned in the North Riding by a Brindle man and Lawrentian missioner, Fr Anselm Bolton. Bolton had served as chaplain at Gilling Castle to the Fairfax family since 1764. He was the last Catholic priest tried for treason, for receiving a dairy maid into the Church, a charge that was of course dismissed. Anticipating her death, and the passing of the property into Protestant hands, the last member of the family, Miss Anne Fairfax, bought up land across the valley from Gilling and built a house which Bolton inhabited from her death in 1793. In 1801 Brewer found Bolton amenable to surrendering his property to his own community, and in the following year he was made Cathedral Prior of Peterborough in recognition of his devotion, and he went to Birtley where he spent the last three years of his life. In December, Prior Appleton and one other priest took up residence at this new house. It was called Ampleforth Lodge.

At this time Lamspring fell victim to the Napoleonic Wars. The last abbot, Maurus Heatley, had followed a very independent policy and Lamspring had drifted apart from the EBC. It had always been separate because of its geographical location, and in its own locality it had a great influence on converting many of the local Lutherans back to Catholicism. But Heatley, after ruling as abbot for forty years, seemed increasingly remote from the young men in his community. A severe row about Heatley's prerogatives with President Brewer in 1801–02 divided and demoralised the community. Heatley died in 1802, and the monastery was taken over by the Prussian government and secularised. They forbade a new election, and closed the school, and prohibited further professions. The monks were given pensions and allowed to live on in peace. For twenty years, some kind of conventual life continued at Lamspring and great courage was shown by some of them in continuing to the end, but the most energetic men passed on to the mission in England, and the others gradually died away. As the school had to be closed, the last novice, Br Clement Rishton, secretly took his vows for St Lawrence's and then led the boys back to England. In April 1803 they were met as they disembarked at Hull and brought to Ampleforth. Three of the oldest boys were clothed later that year as the first generation of novices at Ampleforth: Augustine Baines, Alban Molyneux and Benedict Glover. Rishton himself was ultimately to become prior, Baines a bishop and Molyneux president of the EBC. Thus Ampleforth benefited from the closure of Lamspring.

The survival of St Gregory's at Acton Burnell owed much to the immense generosity of Sir Edward Smythe, who had sheltered them, and to the devotion of two men, Fr Jerome Sharrock and his procurator and successor, Fr Peter Kendal. Sharrock refused the presidency of the EBC in 1799, feeling that his community needed him too much, and in 1806 he refused to become his brother's co-adjutor in the Western District. Two years later he was dead, and Prior Kendal was soon faced with the necessity of moving once more. Sir Edward Smythe died in 1811, and his heir needed the house at Acton Burnell. Prior Kendal at last found and bought Downside House in Somerset, twelve miles south of Bath, which was to be St Gregory's final home.

In Paris, Prior Parker weathered the storms of the Revolution and the rise and fall of Napoleon with extraordinary tenacity, determined to regain and preserve the property of St Edmund's. He spent part of that time in prison, and watched his community dwindle to three priests, and finally by 1814 he was alone. His devotion and serene courage were unrivalled: he saw his monastery rifled, and did all he could to regain his property which he did in 1816 after the Bourbon Restoration, but when he died in 1817 the resident community at St Edmund's became temporarily extinct. A handful of Edmundian priests lived and worked still in England, but there seemed real doubt whether the efforts of Henry Parker would be rewarded.

The Development of the Houses in the first half of the Nineteenth Century

By the middle of the century, the communities had settled in the homes where, for the most part, they stayed. The Brussels nuns had yet to move to East Bergholt from Winchester and ultimately to Haslemere, and the Dunkirk nuns from Hammersmith to Teignmouth; but the Cambray dames settled at Stanbrook in 1838, the Paris community at Colwich in 1836, and the Ghent nuns at Oulton in 1853. The French nuns of Montargis settled at Princethorpe in 1835, where they remained for a hundred and thirty years. The recovery and survival had been remarkable. Not one had been lost.

At first, the situation among the men was far more precarious. Lamspring had no immediate continuity in England, and St Edmund's in Paris also seemed to have died. St Lawrence's had nearly become extinct, saved only by the energy and devotion to his own community of President Brewer. St Gregory's alone survived through its own momentum. It quickly established a pattern of life not dissimilar to that it had kept in France. For a time after moving to Downside, Prior Augustine Lawson was so dissatisfied with the accommodation in the Mendip hills that he planned to return to Douai, but more prudent counsels prevailed and in 1818 a new prior, Fr Bernard Barber, decided to make the future of St Gregory's in Somerset. He ruled at Downside for twelve years and built the first additions to Downside House, a neo-gothic chapel block in 1823. He inherited a school in 1818 with only twenty-four boys, but by 1830 he had increased its size to sixty-two. With great wisdom and strength he resisted the blandishments of Bishop Baines, who wanted to turn Downside into a seminary for the Western District, but after Baines established a fashionable school at Prior Park near Bath with monks and boys from Ampleforth, Downside found it was rivalled in the south by a larger and more aristocratic academy. Most of the Downside boys were tradesmen's sons or else Irish. With Prior Park as a neighbour they could hardly hope to expand, but had to rest content until the second half of the century with about thirty-six boys.

Prior Peter Wilson, during his period of office from 1840 to 1854, presided over a restoration of St Gregory's fortunes. The habit was resumed in 1846 and the cowl in 1850, both of which had been discarded with the French Revolution. In 1854 he put up some new stone buildings and began again the expansion of the school. He had refused an appointment as a bishop in Van Diemen's Land shortly after becoming prior, though in the 1830s and 1840s five Gregorians became bishops, three overseas and two in England.

Developments at Ampleforth were more dramatic. The house taken over from Anselm Bolton soon proved too small, and they gradually extended it on each side and added a top storey, the first of many building mistakes at Ampleforth, as the house was built on a hillside with inadequate foundations. With the young, talented Augustine Baines in charge of the school, still further expansion proved necessary and President Brewer, now the grand old man of the EBC, gave £1,000 of his own money to build a refectory with dormitory and rooms above it behind the old house. In 1818 there were forty-five boys in the school, and it still matched Brewer's original conception of it as a minor seminary preparing boys for the priesthood. They were especially proud of offering Hebrew on the syllabus. The next ten years saw its rapid growth to eighty boys, and the introduction at first under Brewer and Baines and later under Prior Lawrence Burgess of a wholly revolutionary approach to education. Corporal punishment was abolished. The boys were taught modern languages and history as well as the classics by a new technique advocated by a German professor called von Feinagle. Brewer tried unsuccessfully to persuade Downside to accept it also. The school quickly attracted the sons of the gentry and the nobility. It was one of the most fashionable and modern schools in England.

Brewer himself took up residence at Ampleforth in 1818, but

the severity of observance he enjoined did not recommend itself to Prior Burgess. Matins was at 4 a.m., and Brewer made a meditation before that every morning, even though he was then in his late seventies. He insisted upon the full monastic observance of Dieulouard, including enclosure, silent meals, and some kind of habit that consisted of a cassock, scapular and biretta. His final years were soured by quarrels with Burgess, and after a stroke which half paralysed him for a time, he retired to Woolton where he died in 1822. He left his property to Ampleforth, of which he was the greatest and least remembered benefactor.

After President Brewer's death, he was succeeded by Richard Marsh, the last prior of Dieulouard. Marsh and Brewer had worked together in trying to resuscitate St Edmund's, and Marsh had already travelled to France several times to make negotiations about property and the community. He abandoned the idea of continuing St Edmund's in Paris, and favoured rather Prior Parker's suggestion that the community might be re-established in the buildings formerly occupied by St Gregory's at Douai. In 1818, with Parker dead and the Downside community ready to stay in England, Marsh took an Ampleforth junior, Br Charles Fairclough, a protégé of Brewer's, over to Douai to start a school there. At the General Chapter of 1822, however, his proposal to restore St Edmund's at Douai was opposed by Baines and Burgess, who claimed that he had used money belonging to Ampleforth to launch the school there, and who saw little merit in a Benedictine house across the Channel. Marsh went to Rome in 1823 to secure the recognition of the Holy See for the houses in England, and Rome not only acknowledged the monasteries at Downside and Ampleforth and the convent of Cambray nuns at Salford, but also Lamspring, whenever and wherever it might be re-established, and St Edmund's at Douai. Later that year, six young men were clothed for the noviciate at Douai and Marsh, now graced with a Roman doctorate, became the first prior of the revivified community. In 1824 five of the first generation of novices were professed, and three years later one of them, a man of talent who later became a bishop, Fr Bernard Collier, succeeded Marsh as prior.

St Edmund's flourished. The school grew from twenty boys

in 1824 to ninety-five in 1860. A new chapel and refectory were begun in 1840, and further extensions to the school followed. The school was very clerical in character, benefiting from the bursaries granted by the French government to church students in compensation for the seminaries closed in the French Revolution, and many of the boys were destined for the seminaries after leaving. By the end of the century, nearly six hundred priests had been educated there, sixteen of whom became bishops.

Education had become a major work of the EBC in a way that it had not been before the Revolution, and the schools were the mainstay of the Congregation's survival. The first generation of men to grow up in the monasteries restored after the Revolution showed a passionate pastoral interest in education. The greatest of them was Augustine Baines, a handsome and talented man, a brilliant preacher, a man of vision. In 1823 Baines was made co-adjutor of the Western District, and began to develop grand schemes for a school and seminary for his diocese, traditionally the preserve of the Benedictines but also the poorest and least Catholic of the vicariates. He was determined to offer Catholics an education that could rival that of the great schools and the universities from which they were excluded. He sought the help of Downside, asking them whether they would become the school and seminary for his district and thereby detach themselves from the EBC and pass under direct episcopal control. When Prior Barber rejected this offer, Baines turned to his brethren at Ampleforth. Burgess and the others who had done so much to develop the school there under the inspiration of Baines were enthusiastic; they shared his vision and they had already seen something of his flair for success. Baines once more approached Downside, and asked whether they would agree to exchange buildings with the Ampleforth community; Prior Barber, who had just finished building the new chapel at Downside, was loath to move to the North Riding and declined the offer. Baines therefore began to search for property in the Western District which could become a new home for the Ampleforth monks, and he found it near Bath in Ralph Allen's great mansion at Prior Park. In 1829, Baines succeeded as Vicar Apostolic, and his plans proceeded with speed. He persuaded Burgess and the other Ampleforth monks that there was some irregularity in their vows, as Rome had not sanctioned the settlement in England until 1823. He sent a statement of his intentions to Rome, and included this objection to the status of EBC vows within it. Rome replied with a dispensation of Burgess and the other officials, and a *sanatio*, making valid whatever might have been deficient in the professions made in that time. Most of the young men who had at first been impressed by Baines's ideas accepted the *sanatio*, and only the four leading officials and best teachers in the community chose to leave, taking with them about forty boys to Prior Park. There they established a successful school, but Baines's dreams were never realised. One of them, Fr Placid Metcalf, an exceptional linguist, soon changed his mind and asked to return to Ampleforth, but died of plague while awaiting the necessary documents ministering to the poor in Leeds. Baines died in 1843, and Prior Park did not long outlast him. Burgess became in due course second bishop of Clifton, an honour he did not long enjoy as he died exhausted by his efforts to unburden himself of some of the crippling debts of the school.

They left behind them a greatly demoralised community at Ampleforth. There were several years of hard work and real poverty before security and prosperity were at last restored. Educational experiments were abandoned. The school reverted to being a church school, with a large proportion of boys intended for the priesthood. It was the energetic Prior Wilfrid Cooper in the years 1850 to 1863 who matched the work of Prior Wilson at Downside, building the church in 1857 and the new college in 1861, which housed the entire school but was regarded as a great folly of ambitious extravagance that could never be used.

As the houses were becoming more secure, President Austin Birdsall, a Lamspring monk and a successful and conscientious missioner, decided to fulfil the hope expressed in the permission granted by Rome ten years before in re-establishing Lamspring in England in 1834. He chose the quiet mission of Broadway, and at first the community attracted novices. But Birdsall died in 1837, and the new monastery lasted only until 1841.

continued on page 65

A Clothing Ceremony, Ampleforth 1963

Augustine Baker

Dame Gertrude More

Paris, the Monastery

Brindle, founded 1677

The Choir, Lamspring

Goosnargh, founded 1750

Bishop Walmesley

St Gregory's, Douai 1789

Downside c.1840

Bishop Ullathorne

Cardinal Gasquet

Stanbrook

Ampleforth, building the new monastery 1894–98

Cuthbert Butler

St Edmund's at Woolhampton, the Refectory

Belmont

Ampleforth, 1920

Herbert Byrne

Paul Nevill

Downside

St Benet's Hall, Oxford

Belmont, the Abbey Church

Douai, the new cloister

Ampleforth

Buckfast, the Abbey Church

St Louis Priory

Worth Abbey, the Church

Gathering for Community photograph; Abbatial election, Ampleforth 1976

continued from page 40

The difficulties faced by the monasteries on their return to England were largely a reflection of the weaknesses they had already experienced on the Continent. They were overshadowed by the missions, for which they were regarded as seminaries. The senior men in the Congregation mainly lived on parishes. They were hampered by lack of funds. But the Revolution did them the great service of forcing them to face those problems in England rather than in France, and thus to find through their schools a new way of relating to the missionary work of the EBC and a source of new vocations. These were the advantages upon which they were to build in the second half of the century.

Missions Overseas

The Napoleonic wars left England in undisputed control of the Mauritius, Australasia and much of the South Pacific, a part of the world already evangelised by the French and now colonised by many Catholic immigrants, especially Irishmen in Australia. It was clearly desirable for the British government to arrange for the Catholic Church in these territories to be put into the hands of English subjects, especially those areas that had formerly been French and were still subject to the Archbishop of Paris. It was a vast new world, full of promise for the future.

In 1817 Fr Bede Slater, a Lawrentian monk clothed at Acton Burnell, and a nephew of President Bede Brewer, was in Rome negotiating with the curia about the future of Lamspring. As he was one of the few Englishmen available, and as he had come to the Vatican's attention by giving them the false impression that he was an abbot, he was offered the task of becoming the vicar apostolic of the Mauritius, which he accepted with alacrity. He was consecrated as a bishop in Rome, and in letters home described to his uncle his plans for a monastery at the Cape, but President Brewer was reluctant to spare any men at such a difficult time. On returning to England, he raised pensions from the British government and got two monks to accompany him to the Indian Ocean. He set sail in 1820. For all his zeal and forceful personality, he lacked his uncle's financial acumen and received no support from the EBC. His business affairs became a source of scandal and by 1830 Rome had decided to replace him, and asked Prior Barber to undertake the work, but he refused it. In 1832, they offered it to Fr Placid Morris, another Downside monk then on the mission in London, and when he accepted it, Slater was recalled. He had to swim across the harbour at Port Louis to evade his creditors when boarding ship and died during the voyage home.

Morris served in the Mauritius for eight years and was succeeded in 1840 by Fr Bernard Collier, formerly Prior of St Edmund's, who ruled as bishop for twenty-three years, during which time the vicariate became established as the diocese of Port Louis. It remained almost exclusively in the care of the EBC for the rest of the century, almost all the bishops and priests being supplied by Douai. Thus the English Benedictines, for all their early reluctance, were responsible for the creation of the hierarchy in these colonies. Two years after Slater's death, his cousin Fr Bede Polding, another nephew of President Brewer, brought up by him at Woolton but educated at Acton Burnell and a monk of Downside, was chosen by Rome as the Vicar Apostolic of New Holland, for the whole of Australia. Benedictines had served in Australia before, notably Fr Bernard Ullathorne of Downside, but it was fast becoming a major area of settlement, in need of bishops. Polding shared all the qualities of the Brewer clan and the Lancashire middle class: energetic, forceful, solid and not afflicted with scruples. Where Slater had lacked the support he urgently needed in opening fresh territory, Polding received warm encouragement from England, especially from another cousin, Fr Paulinus Heptonstall, a Downside monk who acted as his agent.

By 1842, Polding had created for himself a diocese at Sydney and became its first archbishop, as well as a Count of the Holy Roman Empire. He wanted to establish a Benedictine monastery in Sydney, and entrusted the task to Fr Gregory Gregory as abbot of the Sydney community and vicar general of the diocese from 1848 until 1861. In 1848, with a nun of Stanbrook and a nun of Princethorpe, he also founded a convent at Rydalmere. The convent flourished but the monastery did not. Vocations were not forthcoming from the Catholic settlers, mainly Irishmen.

In 1848 Fr Charles Davis, another Downside monk, was sent

out as co-adjutor to Polding with the title of Bishop of Maitland, but although Polding had already been there for fourteen years, he showed no signs of tiring. Davis died six years later. Twenty years passed before another co-adjutor was appointed, again a Downside monk, Fr Bede Vaughan, the brother of the Cardinal, but it was not until 1877 that he at last succeeded as second Archbishop of Sydney. Polding had ruled there in all for forty-three years. His selfless devotion and evident sanctity made him much loved by his priests and people, and a hundred thousand people took part in the funeral procession. When he had landed in 1835, there had been only six priests in the whole of Australia, but at his death there were five dioceses and a hundred and thirty-five priests in New South Wales alone. One of his most remarkable achievements was the foundation of a major women's order, the Good Samaritans, which came in time to outstrip in size the whole of the EBC, monks and nuns combined. Polding was not merely an activist who thought of nothing but building churches, but a man of prayer and an eloquent critic of contemporary trends, notably the settlers' treatment of the aborigines.

This had been an extraordinary new venture for the EBC. They had never before been so strongly engaged in missionary activity, boldly opening new frontiers. It suited the climate of the age, Victorian optimism and Catholic resurgence, and the apostolic ideals of the EBC. It was underpinned by a revival in the fortunes of the Benedictines in the middle years of the century, and matched by a remarkable development of the parishes that they served in England.

The Development of the Missions

It was another nephew of President Bede Brewer, Fr Anselm Brewer, who began the process of development in the EBC missions in England that was to transform the lives and status of the missioners, to increase the power and importance of the provincials, and to strain the provincial system to its uttermost. In 1838, the year after Anselm Brewer was made Provincial of York, the General Chapter recorded that there were in England and Wales thirty Benedictine missions in all, served by 55 priests. By 1900 the number of missions with resident priests had more than doubled, to sixty-two, and the number of missioners had risen to a hundred and eight. The character of the missions also changed, from quiet, remote one-man missions to large urban parishes with teams of curates, leading quite different lives and facing quite different problems.

Anselm Brewer was one of the boys brought back from Lamspring to finish his education at Ampleforth in 1803. In the year that his uncle died, 1822, he was stationed on one of the largest missions in England, at Brownedge in Lancashire. With the energy and confidence characteristic of his family, he founded a new mission at Clayton Green and built a church there. When Fr Gregory Robinson, the Provincial of the North and formerly the Prior of Ampleforth, died in 1837, Brewer was elected by the priests of the Province to succeed him. He was popular, had the confidence and support of his priests, and presided over the Benedictine parishes of the north at the time of the great influx of Irish immigrants in the 1840s. In the nine years he held office, he supervised in the north the foundation of four new missions, in three of which churches were built, and the building of three new churches in older missions, one of which, St Mary's in Liverpool, was built in unprecedented style at enormous cost. His own grand scheme was the development of a new mission in Liverpool at Edge Hill. He was assured by the EBC representative in Rome that he did not need the bishop's permission to found a new parish, but when his intentions became plain the bishop objected, claiming Rome's sanction for his right to prohibit it. In this state of confusion, Brewer appealed directly to Rome and obtained the necessary permission to found the parish, but he had earned the disfavour of the bishop and aroused the misgivings of his own priests. He then plunged into debt on an unparalleled scale: the mission cost more than £11,000 to develop, in an age when most churches cost a fifth of that sum to build. Brewer completely lost the confidence of the priests of his Province, and was replaced by Fr Alban Molyneux in 1846. His last three years were spent trying to justify his expenditure and his management of the provincial funds, and he died in 1849.

Brewer had vision and flair, but no financial ability. He lacked the security of private means that had made his uncle's rule of the Congregation for almost the first quarter of the century so assured. The Brewer money had passed to Ampleforth, not to the family. He was dealing with far larger sums than any of his predecessors and was trying to move beyond the simple system of domestic account keeping that had satisfied them. He was criticised for employing professional accountants to sort out the muddle. He was not supported in the year after his election in his attempt to start a new missionary fund to finance the development of parishes. He was regarded askance when he tried to found an asylum for prostitutes in Woolton in 1843, though he showed his customary flair in organising a bazaar that raised £1,000. Brewer stood at the watershed. From 1846 onwards, the EBC missions had to change to keep pace with the complete transformation of English Catholic life. Had he been endowed with his uncle's gifts and his uncle's money, and not merely his uncle's boundless self-confidence, he could have shaped the Catholic Church in the north of England. Instead the EBC found that it was itself shaped by developments outside its control.

There was still a large number of one-man missions, but their future was open to doubt. The old style of life, where a missioner might settle for half a century in his quiet rural retreat, was passing. Provincial Athanasius Allanson, who ruled in the north from 1858 until his death in 1876, was one of the last and best examples of the old order. He served the seigneurial mission of the Riddell family at Swinburne in Northumberland for forty-eight years. He was the historian of the EBC, a man of outstanding intelligence, a conservative by temperament and conviction who despaired of the novel features of Catholic life, such as Gothic presbyteries, the re-establishment of the hierarchy, and the primitive monasticism then flourishing on the Continent. He was a Cisalpine of the late eighteenth-century type, fiercely loyal to old privileges and traditions. He was a Catholic example of those clerical scholars who produced massive works of erudition in their country rectories in the years before the reform of the universities in the mid-nineteenth century. He looked back to the world where a mission such as Woolton had been in the hands of President Brewer for forty years and his successor for more than thirty, or where Brindle had been served by only four missioners in a hundred and fifty years between 1721 and 1875. Yet he presided over the northern Province at a time of rapid change, and he saw the world he valued so much disappear.

He organised the Province with faultless efficiency, administering the finances with an exactitude that he had learned through the discipline of historical scholarship. He observed the trend towards larger parishes with teams of curates, but failed to respond to the challenge of finding an appropriate form of monastic life in the new world. The old one-man missions had offered opportunities for solitude and study denied the men in the cities teeming with poor Catholics. The changes in regulations for men living on the mission reflected the inability to deal with the new situation. The first aim was the strengthening of communal life on the larger parishes. In 1854, the General Chapter decreed that any mission with two or more priests should be styled a priory, that the senior priests should be called priors and should be owed obedience by the others, that they should wear the habit and try to observe monastic discipline, and encourage oblates to be attached to the house. This enactment was reformulated less strongly at successive Chapters until 1878, when it was reduced to an exhortation to wear the habit. More practical regulations were drawn up in the north Province in 1858, when it was decreed that all missioners should anticipate Matins and Lauds the night before, should do their half hour of mental prayer before Mass if possible, and give time to study and spiritual reading each day. They were encouraged to write out all sermons, and at least in the first three years after ordination a synopsis should be made. The right to *peculium*, the private property priests needed to be self-sufficient on the mission, was also abolished in 1858, and there were frequent exhortations thereafter in official regulations to observance of poverty on the mission.

All this served to strengthen the power of provincials, especially in matters of finance and the appointment of curates to parishes. But the provincial structure was inadequate to the demands of the time. It failed to provide the necessary context for the development of the monastic missionary ideal. Monks working under conditions of great difficulty in large urban parishes were not offered sufficient monastic identity, and many began to question the need to preserve the provincial structure now that the houses had returned from the Continent. The hollowness of much of the legislation for the parishes in the latter part of the century was apparent in the new regulation of 1883 which chose the eleven largest parishes, those with three or more priests, and called them priories. It was an empty title, an attempt to forestall criticism from the Roman curia and monastic reformers within the EBC. It did not affect the life of the priests or attempt to establish some kind of community life among them, as the measures of thirty years before had tried and failed to do.

Nowhere was the strain of the new situation more apparent than in the great urban mission of St Peter's, Seel Street, in Liverpool. Begun in 1788, it served both the fashionable middle class and the urban poor, and by the 1840s, with the great Irish influx after the famine, it grew into one of the largest parishes in the country. The young priests who left their quiet, rural monasteries to serve there were confronted by problems unknown to their brethren in the villages and small towns of the older missions. Yet they coped superbly, and won the undying affection of their people with their heroism in times of plague, when many of them lost their lives as martyrs of charity, working among the dying and chronically ill in the slums.

The late nineteenth century was an heroic age, with great parish priests struggling to build parishes in the newly expanding cities of industrial England. Of all the great missioners of the century, the greatest was Bernard Ullathorne, a Yorkshireman and Downside monk, born in 1806 and brought up in the spirit of old English recusancy, a descendant of St Thomas More and an adventurous character who went to sea as a cabin boy and voyaged in the Mediterranean and the Baltic before finding his vocation and returning to England to become a monk at Downside. There he made his first Communion at the age of seventeen, and the following year was clothed, the habit used for all the novices simply being placed upon his shoulders symbolically, as the use of the habit had been abandoned with the French Revolution. His novice master was Bede Polding, and his reading was a mixture of French Jansenism, eighteenth-century rationalism, and the Fathers of the Church. He developed the habit he never lost of reading and analysing two or three folio pages each day of one of the Fathers. As a deacon in 1831 he was sent to Ampleforth to take charge of the school after the Baines crisis, but he was not a successful schoolmaster, and the following year, after ordination, he went to Australia as vicar general. The penal settlement was in the middle of transition towards becoming a colony, but he found twenty thousand Catholics, a third of the population, under the care of only three priests. His work in Australia for nine years was an enormous success, especially dealing with the convicts. On his return to England, he was instrumental in influencing the government's policy on transportation.

In 1841 he became the missioner at Coventry. He showed zeal and ability in expanding the parish, building a new church, making many converts. When the new church was consecrated in 1846, he wore the Benedictine habit for the first time since the monks' return to England. His main understanding of his role as a monk-missioner was expressed in this desire to restore some of the externals of monastic observance to the parishes. Throughout his life, he strongly encouraged the surrender of one-man missions by the EBC, and the development of larger urban parishes, small monastic communities that would bring monasticism back into the lives of English Catholics. He was a controversial figure. When he agreed to preach in a Benedictine parish in Liverpool he promised to wear his habit, and received a letter in reply telling him that they would find another preacher.

In 1846 he became vicar apostolic of the Western District, in succession to Bishop Baggs who had himself succeeded Baines two years before. He stood in contrast to his two predecessors as a man of forty, energetic and decisive, of forthright character and tested ability. He moved his place of residence away from Prior Park at once, and withdrew his support from it. Within ten years it collapsed, hopelessly in debt. He preferred to live in Bristol, the largest centre of population in the diocese. In 1850, with the restoration of the hierarchy, he became the first Bishop of Birmingham, a position he held for thirty-eight years. There he befriended

John Henry Newman, whose schemes for a Catholic college at Oxford he warmly supported, and whose views on infallibility he echoed at Vatican I. It was through Ullathorne's intervention that Newman obtained his cardinal's hat in 1879, an action that did not endear him to Cardinal Manning.

He was a great bishop, after Manning the leading bishop in England. He was a learned man and a popular writer, but above all else he was a great monk, a lover of Downside, a warm advocate of monastic life and the monastic service of priests on the mission, a man who, for all the force of his personality and breadth of his experience, yearned for the silence and anonymity of the cloister. Perhaps more than any other man, in the age of the Oxford converts and the Gothic revival, he made Roman Catholicism seem plain and English to his contemporaries. Newman remarked of him in his *Apologia* that if he wanted to point to a straightforward Englishman he would instance the Bishop of Birmingham.

The Development of the Houses in the second half of the Nineteenth Century

The many schemes to unite the houses more closely that had been discussed from before the Revolution had not been forgotten in the early nineteenth century. The tradition of Benedictines supplying bishops for the Western District had been maintained, even in years of some difficulty. These two factors in EBC affairs had run closely together in the premature attempts of Augustine Baines to establish a college and seminary in his diocese with the help of the monks of Downside or Ampleforth. They were fused twenty years later in the foundation of Belmont.

Perhaps the man who did most to bring these ideas to fruition was Fr Joseph Brown of Downside. His ideas were not so remote from those of Baines, but just as Polding succeeded twenty years after Slater because he had the support of the EBC, so Brown's vision proved more timely than Baines's. He had shown early promise in 1829 when he accompanied Richard Marsh to Rome to represent the EBC in the struggle with Baines: it was winter, and he kept warm in the monastery of S. Gregorio while waiting for an interview with Propaganda by skipping; when the Cardinal Prefect heard of this, he granted him an audience at once, and asked for a demonstration. By 1834 he was Prior of Downside, and in 1840 he was made Vicar Apostolic of the Welsh District. He served as bishop in Wales for forty years, and in that time transformed an area that had only seventeen chapels and about five thousand Catholics in 1840 to a population of forty thousand Catholics with forty-seven churches.

In 1850 he became the first Bishop of Newport and Menevia, and in the following year he asked the EBC to form the chapter of his new diocese, after the fashion of the medieval Benedictine cathedrals. Of course, the plan was controversial, doubly so when the idea crystallised into a new monastery that would act as a common noviciate and house of studies for the Congregation, but the offer of Francis Wegg-Prosser, a rich convert, to give land at Belmont in Herefordshire for the foundation was too generous to be refused, and monastic life began there in 1859. From the first, the new noviciate house was regarded with great suspicion by the older missioners, such as Fr Athanasius Allanson, who saw it as a way of introducing strange customs and alien ideas into the EBC. The observance was strict: the regulations drawn up in 1862 emphasised silence, with no talking before lunch, enclosure, and poverty, with nothing allowed in the cells beyond bare necessities. Birettas were not to be worn, and the scapulars were not to have buttons, and thus the EBC habit was settled in its traditional form. But there were complaints about minor points of observance, such as the foreign practice of wearing the amice on the head, or the hours of manual labour that Allanson decried as worthless for English priests, being good only for illiterate monks.

Belmont was ruled by a Cathedral Prior, as the medieval Benedictine cathedrals had been, and the church acted as the cathedral of the diocese. Even the Roman curia, with its long memory, found it difficult to remember what a cathedral prior was supposed to do. The canons of Newport were given the special privilege of wearing fur-trimmed cowls, and in 1891 the Cathedral Prior was granted the use of pontificalia. But for all the archaism, this Benedictine centre played a vital part in Brown's scheme to develop his diocese. Wales almost became a new Benedictine enclave, as many new missions were opened by the other houses. It was also central to the revival of the EBC. The professors were the best in the Congregation, and the standard of studies was very high.

The EBC could not escape the influence of the great monastic revival that had begun on the Continent after the Napoleonic wars. In France, Abbot Prosper Guéranger had created a great centre of liturgical study and strict observance at Solesmes; in Germany, the Wolter brothers conducted another great monastic reform at Beuron. Belmont naturally acted as a vehicle by which these ideas could be interpreted and assimilated by the EBC, while also pursuing a renewed interest in the traditional English spirituality of Augustine Baker. But for the most part, the English monks remained insular. When, for example, Rome introduced new legislation in 1857 creating a new status of simple vows that were a necessary stage before solemn vows could be taken, the EBC did not believe that it could possibly affect them, and continued with solemn professions after one year's noviciate until 1860, when directly ordered by Rome to accept the new regulations.

It was once more the nuns who set the trend for the future. They missed the observance of the choir and the strict enclosure of the monastery far more acutely than the monks after the return to England, and they strove to restore a fuller monastic life. The Cambray nuns resumed the habit in 1823, using patterns supplied by their sisters, the Paris community then at Cannington. When they moved to Stanbrook in 1838, they began a process that took forty years to complete, restoring the church and enclosure that they had enjoyed at Cambray. In 1863 Fr Laurence Shepherd was sent as their new chaplain. He had originally studied theology in Italy, and as novice master at Ampleforth had first begun to use Baker's *Sancta Sophia* as an introduction to the life of prayer. He had continued this at Belmont, where he had been a canon and professor. He was a friend and warm admirer of Abbot Guéranger, and at Stanbrook he translated his *Année Liturgique* in eleven volumes, presenting each of the nuns with a complete set. In the late 1860s a Pugin church was built, and the constitutions drawn up by Guéranger for the French nuns were introduced experimentally at Stanbrook. In 1872 the first Frenchwoman ever to have joined the community, Dame Gertrude Dubois, was elected Abbess, and she proved to be Shepherd's warmest supporter. In 1874 the final permission was granted for the community to adopt the French customs, though not without staunch opposition from a minority of the nuns, and bitter hostility from the more conservative monks. The most significant change was the abandonment of the system of electing abbesses every four years for that of electing life abbesses. The transformation of Stanbrook life was complete in 1878 with the building of a new monastery at the cost of about £12,000, and with it the restoration of full enclosure. These years saw also a rapid increase in the size of the community. Shepherd offered the nuns both the traditional teaching of Baker on the spiritual life and the renewed understanding of the liturgy popularised by Guéranger as the foundation of monastic life. These were to become the cornerstone of the reform of the EBC.

The movement for reform became clearer and more vocal in the late 1870s and early 1880s in Scotland, with the foundation of Fort Augustus. This monastery emerged from two traditions that seemed on the point of dying: the continuation of Lamspring at Broadway, from which a few monks survived working on the mission, and the ancient Scottish Congregation of St James's Abbey, Ratisbon, then represented by one suriving missioner in Scotland, Fr Anselm Robertson. Fr Jerome Vaughan, a Downside monk and professor at Belmont, filled with enthusiasm to ensure the survival of these two communities, was delighted to accept the offer of Lord Lovat's house on the shores of Loch Ness in 1875 as a new monastery for Scotland. Three years later, Vaughan became the first prior of the canonically erected community of Fort Augustus, and Anselm Robertson came to live with him and a few others there. Though Robertson stayed only two years, it was sufficient for Fort Augustus to claim a continuity with the Ratisbon tradition. With strong support from the Scottish aristocracy, Vaughan felt free to introduce continental customs into the house, and after the rapid growth in the monastery's prosperity after Sir David Hunter Blair joined the noviciate, taking the name Br Oswald and bringing his fortune with him,

Fort Augustus aimed at independence from the EBC. Vaughan appealed to Rome. In 1883, at Pontifical High Mass on the feast of the Epiphany celebrated by the Archbishop of St Andrews and Edinburgh, the whole congregation, and not least the two senior councillors acting as his assistants, were astonished when the Archbishop produced a document after the Gospel and read it out: it was a papal brief erecting the monastery as an independent priory, separate from the EBC. The community was wild with rejoicing. A new style of habit and foreign customs were adopted, and four years later Vaughan himself was forced to relinquish his position to the German Prior Leo Linse of Erdington, whom the community chose as prior for life to introduce them into the ways of stricter observance. The following year, Rome made Fort Augustus an abbey, and Linse became life abbot.

The developments in the other houses were far less colourful. They grew steadily in numbers as their schools increased in size, keeping apace with the Catholic revival in England. At Downside, Prior Bernard Murphy began the church, the school refectory block and the monastery, increasing the size of the school from about fifty-five boys to over eighty in 1878. When he was succeeded by Fr Aidan Gasquet as prior in that year, the future of the house was assured. The school at Ampleforth was larger, with ninety-seven boys in 1870, but also far more clerical, for half of that number were church students. The last quarter of the century saw further growth and a rapid decline in the proportion of church students. By the 1890s a magnificent new monastery had been built, and grandiose plans were drawn up for a new church and cloister that were never realised. Despite the extensive building at Douai as the school expanded, by the 1880s it was clear that the intolerance of anti-clerical French governments could force them to return to England, and in 1891 a dependent priory was established at Great Malvern as a possible home for the community. Douai supplied every president of the EBC in the second half of the century.

It was Cuthbert Hedley, though a bishop and a staunch defender of the traditional provincial structure of the missions and of the value of the smaller parishes, who did more than any man to encourage the development of the houses in the last three decades of the nineteenth century. Hedley came from Morpeth, where his father had been a doctor, and was sent to Ampleforth in 1848 at the age of eleven at the instigation of their Benedictine parish priest. He entered the noviciate and continued his studies at Ampleforth under Fr Austin Bury, a brilliant young man fresh from theological studies in Italy, and was set to teach classics in the school when the new college was built in 1861. The following year he was ordained, and soon after sent off to Belmont to become a professor in the new noviciate house. For eleven years he was responsible for the education of young monks, setting the pattern of studies and work and monastic observance that were so severely criticised by the more conservative brethren there. His talents and his warm personality proved themselves, and in 1873 he was consecrated as auxiliary to Bishop Brown, whom he succeeded as bishop of Newport and Menevia in 1881.

As bishop, he both encouraged the development of Belmont and his own community at Ampleforth. Every year, he attended the Exhibition, the prize giving at Ampleforth. In 1895 he persuaded Ampleforth to follow the example of *The Downside Review* and establish *The Ampleforth Journal.* He was a keen journalist, editing *The Dublin Review* even while bishop. He strongly favoured relaxing the restrictions on Catholics attending Oxford and Cambridge and in 1896 was instrumental in opening a Downside house of studies at Cambridge, Benet House, and in 1897 a private hall in the University of Oxford for Ampleforth, St Benet's Hall. Through his guidance and encouragement, the EBC houses entered a new world, with broader horizons, ready to play a significant part in the life of the Church alongside the parishes.

In matters of Congregational reform, Hedley was conservative. He was a strong believer in the provincial system, arguing that as parishes and monasteries have such different aims and belong to such different worlds, they should also have separate superiors. He did not favour the abandonment of smaller parishes to make way for missionary priories of a dozen or more men, and he did not favour the distribution of parishes around the houses of the Congregation, as this could lead to division in the combined missionary effort of the EBC itself. Yet in matters of monastic observance, Hedley belonged to the first generation of reformers, and perhaps his greatest achievement was to present a spirituality founded upon the writings of Augustine Baker that could inspire both the monastic reform and parish priests. The revival of interest in Baker was encouraged at Belmont, where Fr Norbert Sweeney published the first modern English edition of *Sancta Sophia* in 1876. It attracted the interest of monks at Fort Augustus where Fr Benedict Weld-Blundell and Fr Hildebrand Lane-Fox published a variety of excerpts from Baker's writings, and at Downside where Fr Cuthbert Butler and later Fr Hugh Connolly made Baker the basis of their studies into monastic spirituality. At Ampleforth, Fr Ildephonsus Cummins and later Fr Justin McCann published more of Baker's writings and began research into the medieval English mystics.

Hedley died in 1915, having lived long enough to see many of his hopes realised and his fears dispelled. The year before he died, he had seen one of his old students from Belmont, Fr Aidan Gasquet, former Prior of Downside and President of the EBC, rewarded for his scholarly labours with a cardinal's hat. Gasquet was the son of a London doctor, of French émigré stock, and was educated at Downside and became a novice at Belmont in the mid-1860s. He taught in the school for about eleven years until he was elected prior in 1878 at a house election after the resignation of Prior Murphy. He reaped the benefits of Murphy's leadership, presiding over a community of very able men. Feelings of dissatisfaction with the standards of EBC monasticism were galvanised into an ardent spirit of reform when Fr Laurence Shepherd came from Stanbrook in 1882 to preach the community retreat, which he based on Guéranger's monastic ideals. For Gasquet those years also marked the beginning of forty years of friendship and close partnership in historical research with the self-taught, brilliantly learned Edmund Bishop, a layman who remained one of Downside's loyalest friends, eventually providing the basis for a splendid library by bequeathing them his books when he died. In 1884, suddenly afflicted with heart trouble, Gasquet was forced to resign, making way for the election by the young community of its most vigorous reformer, Fr

Edmund Ford. Gasquet retired to London, where he devoted his time to historical research. He evaded the President's design of sending him on the mission by securing a papal brief authorising him to continue to work in London through the intervention of Cardinal Manning, to whom he was related by marriage, and thus began a career in historical scholarship which made Gasquet a name familiar to every enthusiast for medieval and Tudor history.

Gasquet had flair, drive, and above all the example and encouragement of Edmund Bishop. He produced a succession of enormously successful historical works. By 1900 he had been appointed President of the EBC; in 1903 his name, along with Hedley and the young Bishop Bourne of Southwark, headed the list sent to Rome recommending a successor to Cardinal Vaughan at Westminster. To the surprise of all, Bourne was appointed. But Gasquet found his reward in 1912, when he was made chairman of the Pontifical Commission engaged in revising the Vulgate Bible, and in 1914 he was made a cardinal.

Gasquet had risen to great eminence, but even in his own lifetime his historical research came under attack. He had undertaken work on the middle ages and the Tudors just as the academic study of history at the universities was beginning to replace the amateur studies of antiquarians. He lacked the rigour of professional historians; he had an unusual tendency to be inaccurate, and was such a popular writer that he was always catering for the market, never revising, but publishing as fast as possible. In his old age, he was made Prefect of the Vatican Archives, dying in Rome in 1929.

New Ventures

Reformed continental monasticism influenced English religious life in the second half of the century through foundations that offered an alternative to the EBC. The Italian Cassinese monks of the primitive observance emphasised austerities such as a night office and abstinence from meat most days in the week. They attracted young Englishmen into their cloisters after 1848 when they began to supply Archbishop Polding with missionaries in Australia. Among the first were Anselm O'Gorman, an old boy of Douai School, who later transferred to the EBC of which he ultimately became President, and Wilfrid Alcock, a Lancastrian and old Amplefordian. In 1861 the Cassinese made a foundation at Ramsgate in Kent, which became part of the new Subiaco Congregation in 1867, formed from a federation of the Cassinese of the primitive observance and the monasteries of La Pierre qui Vire in France and Montserrat in Spain. They opened a school which showed early promise, and in 1872 Wilfrid Alcock was elected as first ruling Benedictine abbot in England since Feckenham. He was not a good administrator, and the community did not flourish. He was deposed by Rome in 1876, and went to Australia and New Zealand as a missionary. Ramsgate remained a priory until 1896, and long kept its early missionary flavour, with parochial commitments, convent chaplaincies and the school and links with the foreign missions. In 1904 Fr Ambrose Agius was made an archbishop as Apostolic Delegate to the Philippines. They entered the twentieth century not unlike the EBC houses, still largely unaffected by the liturgical movement.

The great German reform movement of the Wolter brothers at Beuron and Maredsous stressed the importance of the liturgy and adherence to the Rule in Benedictine life. Beuron founded a priory at Erdington near Birmingham in 1876, and several talented Englishmen who had joined Maredsous in Belgium were transferred there, notably Fr John Chapman. Erdington's influence was not proportionate to its size; Fort Augustus took Leo Linse as its first abbot, and after the anti-German feeling of the First World War swept away the German community most of the English brethren joined other communities; Chapman eventually became Abbot of Downside.

Anti-clericalism in France led La Pierre qui Vire to make a foundation at Buckfast in Devon in 1882. It became independent in 1899 and was made an abbey in 1902. After the tragic accidental death of its first abbot, the community flourished under the thirty-two year abbacy of one of the greatest Benedictines of the century, Anscar Vonier. The monks of Solesmes sought refuge on the Isle of Wight in 1906 at Quarr, where they built a magnificent new monastery as a temporary residence that eventually became an independent abbey. They had already accepted the church at Farnborough where Napoleon III was buried and established a monastery in 1895 that became an abbey in 1903. Farnborough, under its first abbot, Fernand Cabrol, gained a reputation as one of the greatest communities of scholars in the world. Cabrol, Fr Henri Leclercq and Fr André Wilmart are remembered as liturgical scholars and historians of rare erudition.

These developments even touched the Church of England. In 1868 a community of Anglican nuns living a strict Benedictine life was set up; for many years it was at West Malling and later at Milford Haven. After 1870, some kind of Benedictine life was followed at Llanthony in Wales by Ignatius of Jesus, but his influence was not as great as that of Aelred Carlyle who founded a community on the Isle of Dogs in 1896 that moved to Caldey in 1906. There they lived an austere, simple, Cistercian-like life until 1913 when both they and the nuns at Milford Haven under their abbess, Scholastica Ewart, were received into the Catholic Church. For a time, the monks at Caldey were put into the hands of John Chapman from Erdington. They later moved to Prinknash. One oblate of Caldey, Denys Prideaux, remained an Anglican and founded another Anglican community at Pershore which later moved to Nashdom. It was different from Caldey, taking its character from Prideaux as its abbot, being intellectual and scholarly and greatly influenced by French monasticism. The nuns had to move in 1919 to Talacre in Wales, to the family home of their patron, Bishop Mostyn, and two years later they sought admission to the EBC.

Thus the early years of the twentieth century saw the EBC no longer unrivalled by other kinds of monasticism. As the EBC houses asserted their independence of congregational structures and began to restore much that had been lost in the last years of the eighteenth century and through the French Revolution, they could not but be affected by the example and inspiration of these impressive, though different, traditions.

Congregational Reform

The last quarter of the nineteenth century saw a fierce dispute about the nature of the EBC arising from the very success of two distinct trends in its development in the middle years of the century: the larger parishes and stronger provincial structure, and the growing self-sufficiency of the monasteries and yearning for independence and monastic reform. The quarrel centred on the provincial system. The reformers wanted to abolish the provinces, and attach the parishes to the monasteries; the conservatives wanted to preserve the parishes from control by the superiors in the monasteries, because they feared that the parishes would be restricted in the hands of men with different aims from the mission fathers. Behind this issue lay the deeper question of the real nature of the EBC: was it a missionary body, with monasteries as seminaries for the missions, or a real monastic congregation, of autonomous, reformed monastic houses?

The dispute came to the surface in 1880, when long-standing disagreements between the EBC and the bishops were resolved by the Roman decree *Romanos Pontifices*; interest had been aroused in the nature and affairs of the EBC in Rome, and the curia's natural dislike for anomalies was fortified by the fact that every member of the English hierarchy had expressed the view that the EBC needed reform. In 1881 the claustral Prior of Monte Cassino, Boniface Krug, was sent to make a visitation of the English monasteries. Krug was a German American, originally a monk at St Vincent's, Latrobe, under Abbot Boniface Wimmer, and later a monk of Monte Cassino in Italy where he had been prior for eleven years. Krug spent six months visiting all the monasteries in England, and many of the parishes, drawing up a careful report of what he found in the EBC. At Downside under Gasquet and Fort Augustus under Vaughan, he found widespread dissatisfaction with the system of congregational government. At Ampleforth and Douai, he met with strongly conservative views, and at Belmont he found opinions more divided. On returning to Rome, he therefore proposed that the EBC should try to define its aims more clearly, that the houses should be erected into abbeys, that Downside should have its own noviciate, that Fort Augustus should be made independent, but that the missions should be kept.

During the inevitable pause while Rome decided how to act, a virulent pamphlet war followed during most of 1882. The three most prominent conservatives were Fr Benedict Snow, a

Downside monk who had served the Liverpool missions for 26 years and was in turn procurator and then Provincial in the north; Fr Bede Prest, formerly Prior of Ampleforth, who had served on several of the Lancashire missions; and Fr Austin Bury, an Ampleforth monk and contemporary of Laurence Shepherd, who had studied with him in the 1840s and was regarded as one of the most learned Thomists in England, as well as a fluent Italian speaker who wrote several pamphlets in Italian and translated others for the benefit of the curia, and who had served several parishes in the north, becoming Provincial of York. The men ranged against them were younger, less well known, but not less determined. Their main spokesman was Mgr Weld, a secular priest and great benefactor of Downside.

The conservatives felt that they had won when Rome's decision was published. The rescript *Cliftonien* of 1883 changed practically nothing. It ordered that the Constitutions should be revised, that missioners should return every sixth year to their monasteries for three months, and that the superiors, including the provincials, should live in the monasteries, and that the General Chapter should include only men exercising jurisdiction. Clearly, Rome was attempting to give greater weight to the monasteries, and subject the parishes to them, but the EBC were baffled at the imprecise and confusing orders. The dilemma was resolved by naming the eleven largest parishes priories and regulating that henceforth the provincials and president should live in these. They decided that the regulation regarding the composition of General Chapter could also be ignored in the case of the Cathedral Priors, even though seven of the twelve holding these titular dignities in 1883 did not have other appointments that would entitle them to a seat. Thus the conservative composition of the Chapter was not threatened. To make their triumph complete, the conservatives elected Fr Anselm O'Gorman as president, a man who had tasted the reform in his youth as a monk in the Subiaco Congregation and had later transferred to Douai.

1883 also saw the withdrawal of Fort Augustus from the EBC and the complete victory there of the young reformers led by Vaughan. The vanguard of the reform was therefore left to

Downside, and after 1885 to the tireless energy and idealism of Prior Edmund Ford. When Ford realised that the proposed revision of the Constitutions was to be entrusted to a small group of missioners he appealed unsuccessfully to Rome. Fr Cuthbert Butler, an able young priest at Downside, wrote a short book, *Notes on the Origin and early Development of the Restored EBC 1600–1661* (1887), which showed that the EBC was a monastic and not simply missionary body from its inception. But the new Constitutions were a complete expression of conservative views, and they gained Rome's approval. In 1888 O'Gorman was succeeded by another Edmundian as president, Fr Austin O'Neill, and the Chapter replaced Ford with Fr Clement Fowler. When a formal protest was lodged against this appointment by Downside, O'Neill had to go to Rome to justify the reforms and recent development of the EBC at the Vatican. There he was dismayed to discover that the curia had intended to have the provincial system dismantled and the missions shared out between the houses. Rome confirmed Fowler in his appointment, but O'Neill loyally returned and explained the Vatican's views. Ampleforth and Douai quickly accepted the new policy, but strong opposition was still voiced at the General Chapter of 1889, where the proposed reform was defeated by one vote. The old cisalpine spirit was not dead.

This provoked Rome to intervene once more in 1890 with the decree *Religiosus Ordo*, abolishing the provincial system and sharing the parishes between Downside, Ampleforth and Douai. Yet still the conservatives refused to accept that further reform was needed: an extraordinary General Chapter in 1892 failed to make any alteration in the status of the houses. In 1895 Rome intervened again, sending Fr Hildebrand de Hemptinne, the first Abbot Primate, to conduct a visitation. During the long wait while Rome considered his report, O'Neill became Bishop of Port Louis and O'Gorman once more became President. Thus it fell to him to implement the Roman decision *Diu Quidem* in 1899, which drastically reduced the size of the Chapter to the superiors of the houses, delegates from each and three other officials. The three priories were erected into abbeys, with abbots to be elected for life, but only for eight years in the first instance, a provision which became normal. During the Chapter that enacted this legislation, President O'Gorman resigned and was succeeded by Fr Aidan Gasquet. Thus he presided as the first abbots were elected in 1900, Fr Edmund Ford at Downside, Fr Oswald Smith at Ampleforth and Fr Lawrence Larkin at Douai. In 1901, Belmont was allowed to take novices for itself, thus becoming a fourth independent house with an Ampleforth monk, Fr Ildephonsus Cummins, as prior.

The resolution of the bitter disputes that ended the nineteenth century saw the victory of the ideals and vision that had been most closely identified with Downside and above all with its patient and determined superior, Edmund Ford. Downside had led the movement for reform of congregational government; it now continued to lead the movement towards fuller monastic reform.

CHAPTER THREE: THE TWENTIETH CENTURY

1900 marked a watershed for the EBC. By reducing the size and authority of the General Chapter and the powers of the President and by distributing the parishes between the houses, there was a new emphasis on the independence of the monasteries that opened the way to their fuller development. The first forty years of the century set the pattern for the second forty; by the Second World War the main lines had already been drawn: new foundations, growth in numbers, larger schools, openness to the world and fuller monastic observance.

As the provinces were abolished and the missions distributed between the houses, all monks in the Congregation were now directly under the authority of the abbots or priors of the communities for which they had been clothed. It made far less difference to the parishes than the conservatives had feared. The traditional Benedictine enclaves in Lancashire, west Cumberland, Northumberland and South Wales remained long unaffected, and were only gradually handed over to the dioceses. The spirit and unity of Benedictine parishes belonging to whatever abbey remained unimpaired, still supported for another generation by the experience of the common noviciate at Belmont. In 1898 there were seventy-eight EBC parishes, and in 1935 the number still stood at seventy-six. Downside surrendered more than half its parishes, but Douai and Belmont increased their parochial commitments. In the last twenty years, the parishes have declined in numbers; in 1979 there were thirty-eight missions with resident priests.

The parishes retained their united identity for many years because of the common noviciate at Belmont, but the new autonomy of the houses soon demanded the setting up of separate noviciates. Downside withdrew from Belmont in 1908, and the other houses after the First World War. This left Belmont free to develop as an independent house, becoming an abbey in 1920 and opening its school to non-Church students in 1926. The houses opened for study in the universities, by Downside at Cambridge in 1896 and by Ampleforth at Oxford in 1897, still provided a common meeting ground for monks from different communities, as men from all the monasteries were sent to university to gain degrees to teach in their schools. The experience of university education and theological study abroad, in the new Benedictine college of Sant' Anselmo in Rome or in the Catholic universities at Fribourg and Louvain, did more than anything else to change the character of the houses, with their renewed intellectual vigour and higher academic standards in their schools. A remarkable renaissance in scholarship and theology affected every house in the EBC, and especially Downside where the establishment of *The Downside Review* in 1880 was an early intimation of its later reputation for learning. The literary output of EBC monks in the twentieth century has been exceptional, with a distinguished contribution to historical, theological and spiritual studies. Men such as Cuthbert Butler, Benedict Mackay, John Chapman, Stephen Marron, Hugh Connolly, David Knowles, Justin McCann and John Stéphan established their reputations in a variety of fields and set a pattern that their successors have followed.

The return to fuller monastic observance was pioneered at Downside by Abbot Cuthbert Butler, an Irishman, educated at Downside and clothed at Belmont in 1876. His early years at Downside were marked by the great constitutional crisis, in which he was a keen advocate of reform. His early promise as a scholar was at last rewarded in 1896 when he was sent to found Benet House at Cambridge, where he worked for eight years to produce a new and definitive text of an early monastic work, the *Lausiac History*. He was elected abbot in 1906 and followed a policy of fostering Downside's development in pursuit of scholarship and liturgical excellence, together with the expansion of the school under Fr Leander Ramsay. For the first time since the French Revolution, he introduced more singing into the Office and Mass with the new style of Solesmes plainchant, and greater beauty in vestments and the furnishings of the church. His conception of monastic life was presented in two great books, the fruit of time snatched from the busy hours of administration, both as Abbot and as President of the EBC. In 1919 he wrote *Benedictine Monachism*, an essay on the monasticism of St Benedict and its historical development, and a handbook of the monastic reform, and in 1922 he wrote *Western Mysticism*, an attempt to trace through St Augustine, St Gregory the Great and St Bernard a monastic mystical tradition in the West. With typical humility, he was persuaded to revise the book, writing a new chapter and re-arranging the material. His text of the *Rule of St Benedict* remains, for all practical purposes, unsurpassed. He was a man of enormous intelligence and utmost, almost eccentric, regularity in prayer, administration, study and manual labour. Having resigned in 1922 over the policy of surrendering parishes, he spent the last twelve years of his life at Downside's foundation at Ealing, where he devoted himself to writing, lecturing and speaking in Hyde Park.

Butler's work as abbot was matched by Fr Leander Ramsay's work as headmaster, building up the school to provide a work for a growing community. A convert with a distinguished academic reputation, Ramsay's research into St Cyprian was cut short in 1902 by his appointment as headmaster, an office he held for sixteen years. He inherited a school of about a hundred and twenty boys, and left it a school of about four hundred. He was the first man to bring a Benedictine school into line and into competition with the non-Catholic public schools, and earned for Downside a place among the great schools of the country. After a few years as novice master, he succeeded Butler as abbot in 1922, but never lived to complete his first term of office. He continued Butler's work, completing the nave of the abbey church and setting a standard of observance that was an inspiration to his monks. His successor, Abbot John Chapman, was another brilliant convert and originally a monk of Maredsous. He was a notable patristic and scriptural scholar, but is best remembered today for his posthumous *Spiritual Letters*. The growth of Downside in these years was marked by two foundations, at Ealing, begun as a parish in 1897 and made a dependent priory twenty years later, and at Worth in Sussex in 1933. The latter foundation was not made without dispute at Downside, and there was controversy on the future of the community that led finally to one of the most gifted of the rising generation of priests, Fr David Knowles, severing his links from Downside and becoming a don at Cambridge. Knowles, perhaps more than any other man, symbolised the Downside spirit of scholarship, making medieval monastic history a major area of historical research.

These developments at Downside were mirrored in the changes taking place in the other houses. The Association Laws in France forced St Edmund's to return to England from Douai in 1903, as they had long foreseen. Initially, there was some uncertainty whether to settle at Woolhampton in Berkshire; many of the community wanted to move to the North, but the purchase of more land and the gradual extension of the buildings persuaded them to stay. As the bursaries provided by the French government were no longer available, the school had to be turned into a modern public school. The great architect of the transformation was Fr Ignatius Rice, headmaster for thirty-seven years, 1915–1952. He was a sportsman as well as a literary man and friend of Chesterton and Belloc, a headmaster who influenced many generations of boys by his courtesy and his kindness as well as his towering personality and exceptional mind. Douai's stability can be gauged from the forty-year abbacy of Fr Sylvester Mooney, from 1929 to 1969. The school was not allowed to grow to the point where it lost completely its old intimacy, and perhaps this contributed to the community's reputation for friendliness.

In 1909 Fort Augustus returned to the EBC, and opened a small school soon after. Its history, and the Congregation's, took a different turn when Fr Leonard Sargent, an American who had made his noviciate at Downside, opened a monastery at Portsmouth, Rhode Island in America in 1919. This inspired a group to ask Fort Augustus to make a foundation at Washington in 1924, and two years later Portsmouth was also put into the hands of Fort Augustus. Both communities flourished, establishing highly successful schools, and by the late 1930s they had both become predominantly American. They earned a reputation for strict observance and scholarship, and the Washington monks taught in the Catholic university of America nearby.

The return of Fort Augustus brought also the convent that they had founded on the shores of Loch Ness. In 1917, under Dame Scholastica Weld, they became an abbey, and under Dame Cecilia Carmont, who was Abbess from 1919 until 1965, the nuns moved to Holme Eden near Carlisle in 1921. In that same year Talacre entered the EBC, to be followed by Colwich in 1926 after nearly three hundred years of independence. Two years later, Colwich was also made into an abbey. By 1930 there were two hundred nuns in the four convents in the EBC, though they were still only a minority of the Benedictine nuns in England. Stanbrook remained the largest house, and gained a reputation throughout the world for printing; begun in 1876 at the instigation of Fr Laurence Shepherd, the Stanbrook press was used to print books for the Congregation at first, copies of the Rule and rituals, and, after changing fortunes in the twentieth century, underwent a renaissance in the 1950s. Work printed by the nuns has been exhibited all over the world, and the press is now believed to be one of the oldest and one of the finest private presses in England.

The 1920s and 1930s also saw a rapid growth in the size of the monastery and school at Ampleforth during the abbacy of Fr Edmund Matthews, 1924–1939. He was the first Benedictine to have taken a degree at Oxford since the Reformation, and dreamed of developing a large, modern public school at Ampleforth. But he had to struggle to save the school from near collapse as headmaster after the First World War. As abbot, he was fortunate to find a team of gifted young monks eager to fulfil his aims for the school, among whom Fr Paul Nevill proved to be one of the greatest headmasters of the century. Paul Nevill had become a novice at Belmont in 1899, at the age of seventeen. He took his vows in the year Ampleforth became an abbey, and then read History at Oxford. He always had a pragmatic mind, a man of hard common sense, but he was above all a man of vision, a man utterly consumed by the idea of turning Ampleforth into one of the great English schools, emulating the work of Fr Leander Ramsay and his successors at Downside. He was tall, of commanding bearing, a natural leader. In his thirty years as headmaster, from 1924 until his death, at his desk, in 1954, he quadrupled the size of the school, established a strong house system to preserve its family spirit, and earned a very high reputation for Ampleforth in studies and games.

By 1939 the transformation had already taken place, and the work of consolidation fell to Abbot Herbert Byrne, who ruled for twenty-four years, from 1939 until 1963. He had been on a parish for four years in Liverpool when he was elected, aged fifty-four, and long remained convinced that he was a square peg in a round hole, yet he was twice re-elected and only resigned when he was seventy-eight. His courtesy, genial good humour mixed with dour pessimism but enlivened with an exceptional wit, his deep love for his brethren and his profound stability in manner and in purpose won the respect and loyalty of the community. He could be very severe, and severest of all with himself. He ruled at Ampleforth during the years when it became one of the largest monasteries in Europe and one of the biggest schools in England, but he did most of his work without a secretary, even as President between 1941 and 1961, with an energy envied by many younger men. When they were building the abbey church at Ampleforth, and he was in his mid-seventies, he was quite capable of returning from a long walk and at once making the difficult ascent to the top up awkward ladders. At seventy-eight, he did not retire, but became a curate on the mission at Leyland, where he worked for fifteen years, greatly loved by the people, until his last illness and death at the age of ninety-four in 1978.

The monasteries in the other congregations in England shared in these years of growth and expansion. Ramsgate, with its school and parish commitments and convent chaplaincies, seemed rather remote from Prinknash, with its primitive observance, its craft and field work, its white habit as a sign of its Cistercian spirit, and from Buckfast, where the monks built their magnificent neo-gothic abbey church by hand, and which was gaining an international reputation for bee keeping, stained glass making, and tonic wine. Yet the three houses, all members of the Subiaco Congregation, came together to form an English province in 1938. The most distinguished monk in the three houses was Abbot Anscar Vonier of Buckfast, a theologian of exceptional insight and an abbot of great strength and vision. Quarr, even after the Solesmes community returned to France, continued to flourish; in 1925 it became a priory and in 1937 an abbey. It gradually lost its French character, but retained the strict observance, the beautiful plainchant and the scholarly tradition it had inherited from Solesmes. But the appeal of Farnborough, a scholarly community without rival, was more narrow, and lack of vocations led the Solesmes Congregation to hand it over to Prinknash, who established a dependent priory there in 1947 which was made independent in 1969. The following year, Prinknash made a foundation in Scotland at Pluscarden, which eventually became an abbey in 1974. Ramsgate, through the work of Fr Bede Winslow, became a centre of ecumenism long before most Catholics had ever heard the word. In 1936 two new communities were founded in London, both with a strong social and missionary dimension: a mission house for the St Ottilien Congregation, German Benedictine missionaries, at Hendon, and a double monastery for men and women at Cockfosters by the Olivetan Congregation, who already had a convent at Ravenswood in Kent.

Until the start of the twentieth century, almost all the houses of nuns, whether part of the EBC or not, were part of the same tradition, but the anti-clericalism that brought several communities of men to England from France also brought greater variety among the nuns. A French community established on the Isle of Wight in 1882 moved to Ryde forty years later and became an abbey in 1926. As they were near Quarr, they became part of the Solesmes Congregation in 1950. A convent was opened by them in India in 1967, the first for Indian Benedictines. A community consecrated to the Sacred Heart moved from Paris to Tyburn in 1903, where they prospered and later made foundations in Australia and Peru. Some convents closed their schools: Princethorpe closed theirs in 1966 and moved to Fernham; Oulton closed theirs in 1969 and opened a guest house. The convent founded by Bede Polding in Australia found a new home at Pennant Hills in

1957. Sadly, the oldest English convent of all, the Brussels nuns of East Bergholt, even though they moved to Haslemere after the Second World War, had to be closed in 1976 through lack of vocations, and the nuns settled in other communities.

The new foundations in the EBC gained their independence in the 1940s and 1950s: Ealing, Washington, Portsmouth and Worth were all vigorous, new communities, smaller than their parent houses and perhaps more ready to adapt to new conditions. Buckfast chose to join the English Congregation in 1960, and opened a preparatory school. Ampleforth made a foundation at St Louis in 1955 that gained its independence in 1973. A sign of the changing climate of the age was building. Downside and Buckfast built two of the finest neo-gothic churches in England in the 1930s, taking years of labour and finally furnishing them with traditional care. Ampleforth also built a neo-gothic church, finished in 1961, the very year that a revolutionary new church was constructed for their foundation at St Louis, a round building of concrete and glass. The contrast marked the watershed of the 1960s. When Worth came to build their church in the 1970s, they too built it round, with the emphasis upon flexibility in use rather than splendour.

With the Vatican Council, a new mood swept the EBC. It was fortunate to have as President the Abbot of Downside, Christopher Butler, a brilliant convert and distinguished theologian who attended the Council as President and was one of the most influential English-speaking members. In 1966, he became auxiliary bishop of Westminster. Reform was again in the air, and a new generation of abbots emerged to lead their communities through the difficult years of adaptation, one of the best known of whom was Fr Basil Hume of Ampleforth, the successor of Herbert Byrne, who was Abbot from 1963 until he became Archbishop of Westminster in 1976. In many cases, the impetus of reform and change passed to the smaller and newer abbeys. New initiatives were taken in communal work, such as the lay communities established by several monasteries, notably Worth, where lay people live and work and pray alongside the monks, or such as the missions abroad, especially Worth's foundation in Peru. Perhaps the biggest changes were liturgical, making the differences between the houses more apparent as each adapted its office to its own needs.

Yet in many ways the new ideas of Vatican II were not strange to the EBC. With its tradition of independent monasteries, an emphasis on decentralised authority was not difficult to accept. With its elected abbots and its tradition of rugged individualism, a new emphasis on authority listening to those it served caused no surprise. The opening of the scriptures, the return to a simple spirituality and life-style in the Church were a rediscovery that the Benedictine life had long enshrined.

The English Benedictines entered the 1970s with a new relevance to a Church in England that they had not only served for many centuries, helped shape and develop from the time of St Augustine and again through the dark years of recusancy and the revival of the nineteenth and twentieth centuries, but a Church that once more looked to its roots for inspiration and guidance for the future.

BIBLIOGRAPHY

History

Archives:

Each house has a store of archives relating to its history; the fullest is at Downside, where the Congregational archives are kept. Much pre-Revolutionary material was left on the Continent.

Manuscript: of particular significance are the following:

Dom Bennet Weldon, *Memorials to help the writing of the history of the Benedictine Order renewed in England* 2 vols (1707), at Douai.

Dom Athanasius Allanson, *A History of the English Benedictine Congregation, 1585–1850* 14 volumes (1843–1858), at Ampleforth, copies at Downside. Now available on microfiches, edited with introduction by Dom Placid Spearritt and Dom Bernard Green, Oxford 1978.

Dom Basil Whelan, *Annals of the English Congregation of the Black Monks of St Benedict, 1850–1900* 2 vols (1932), in most house archives.

Dom Justin McCann, *Annals of the English Benedictine Congregation, 1840–1901* (1942), in most house archives.

D. M. Lunn, *The Origins of the EBC, 1588 – 1647* (unpublished Cambridge PhD thesis, 1970).

Reference:

Dom Norbert Birt, *Obit Book of the English Benedictines, 1600–1912*, Edinburgh 1913 (marred by many inaccuracies).

Dom Basil Whelan, *A Series of Lists relating to the English Benedictine Congregation*, Stanbrook 1933.

List of Boys at St Gregory's, Downside 1972.

Bullarium Monachorum Nigrorum S. Benedicti Congregationis Angliae, Fort Augustus 1912.

The Benedictine Yearbook (formerly, *The Benedictine Almanack and Guide*) is published annually.

Periodicals:
The Downside Review, The Ampleforth Journal, The Ampleforth Review, and *The Douai Magazine* contain many invaluable articles, too numerous to list. Of particular significance are the following:
Vincent Marron, 'Some Sources for English Benedictine History', *The Downside Review,* vol 81, 1963, pp 50–60.
Dom Philip Jebb, 'The Archives of the English Benedictine Congregation. Kept at St Gregory's, Downside' *The Downside Review,* vol 93, 1975, pp 208–225.

Dom David Knowles, *The Religious Orders in England,* vol 3, Cambridge 1959.
Dom Yves Chaussy, *Les Bénédictins Anglais Réfugiés en France au XVIIe siècle 1611–1669,* Paris 1967.
Dom Justin McCann, *English Benedictine Missions, a Survey,* privately printed, 1940.
Dom Gilbert Dolan, *Lancashire and the Benedictines,* privately printed, 1898.
T. P. Ellis, *The Welsh Benedictines of the Terror,* Newtown 1936.
ed Dom Justin McCann and Dom Hugh Connolly, *Memorials of Fr Augustine Baker and other Documents relating to the English Benedictines, Catholic Record Society,* vol 33, London 1933.
ed Dom Justin McCann, *Life of Fr Augustine Baker O.S.B. (1575–1641)* by Peter Salvin and Serenus Cressy, London 1933.
Dom Bernard Ullathorne, *From Cabin Boy to Archbishop (ed* Shane Leslie) London 1941.
Dom Bernard Ullathorne, *Letters* (ed Mother F. R. Drane, O.S.D.), London 1892.
Dom Cuthbert Butler, *The Life and Times of Bishop Ullathorne* 2 vols, London 1926.
Dom Norbert Birt, *Benedictine Pioneers in Australia* 2 vols, London 1911.
Dom Anselm Wilson, *The Life of Bishop Hedley,* London 1930.
Shane Leslie, *Cardinal Gasquet,* London 1953.
Nigel Abercrombie, *The Life and Work of Edmund Bishop,* London 1959.

Dom Bruno Hicks, *Hugh Edmund Ford,* London 1947.
Dom David Knowles, *The Historian and Character,* Cambridge 1963 (for studies of Gasquet and Cuthbert Butler).
Dom Adrian Morey, *David Knowles, a Memoir,* London 1979.
Dom Norbert Birt, *A History of Downside School,* London 1902.
Dom Benedict Snow, *Sketches of Old Downside,* London 1903.
Dom Hugh Connolly, *Some Dates and Documents for the Early History of our House,* privately printed, 1930.
Dom Hubert van Zeller, *Downside By and Large,* London 1954.
Dom Augustine James, *The Story of Downside Abbey Church,* Downside 1961.
Dom Cuthbert Almond, *The History of Ampleforth Abbey,* London 1903.
ed Dom Justin McCann and Dom Columba Cary-Elwes, *Ampleforth and its Origins,* London 1952.
Dom Cuthbert Doyle, *The Tercentenary of St Edmund's,* London 1917.
Dom Basil Whelan, *The History of Belmont Abbey,* London 1959.
ed Joseph Gillow, Cambray nuns 'Records, 1620–1793' in *Catholic Record Society* vol 13, 1913, pp 1–85.
Benedictines of Stanbrook, *In a Great Tradition,* London 1956.
Benedictines of Stanbrook, *Stanbrook Abbey Press,* Stanbrook 1970.
ed Joseph S. Hansom, Paris nuns 'Notes and Obituaries, 1652–1861' in *Catholic Record Society* vol 9, 1911, pp 334–431.
Robert Eaton, *The Benedictines of Colwich, 1829–1929,* London 1929.

Spirituality and Monastic Theology

A Monk of Ampleforth (i.e. Abbot Herbert Byrne) *St Benedict and the Benedictine Life* CTS/B475.
Dom Augustine Baker, *Sancta Sophia* (1657); new ed, with introduction by Dom Gerard Sitwell, *Holy Wisdom,* Wheathampstead 1972.
Dom Augustine Baker, *The Confessions of Venerable Fr Augustine Baker O.S.B.,* ed Dom Justine McCann, London 1922.

Dom Augustine Baker, *The Inner Life and Writings of Dame Gertrude More,* 2 vols, ed Dom Benedict Weld-Blundell, London 1910 – 11.

Dom Cuthbert Butler, *Benedictine Monachism*, London 1919.

Dom Cuthbert Butler, *Western Mysticism,* 2nd ed with afterthoughts, London 1927.

Dom David Knowles, *The Benedictines*, London 1929.

Dom Cuthbert Butler, *Ways of Christian Life*, London 1932.

Dom John Chapman, *Spiritual Letters*, London 1935.

Dom Hubert van Zeller, *The Holy Rule*, London 1958.

Dom Hubert van Zeller, *The Benedictine Idea*, London 1959.

Dom Christopher Butler, *Prayer, an Adventure in Living,* London 1961.

Dom Hubert van Zeler, *Approach to Monasticism,* London 1963.

Dom Hubert van Zeller, *The Benedictine Nun*, Dublin 1965.

Dom Columba Cary-Elwes, *Monastic Renewal*, New York, 1967.

Dom Aelred Graham, *The End of Religion*, London 1971.

Dom Christopher Butler, *A Time to Speak*, Southend on Sea, 1972.

Dame Maria Boulding, *Contemplative Nuns, are they wasting their lives?,* CTS/H464 (1973).

Dom Illtyd Trethowan, *Mysticism and Theology*, London 1975.

Dom Basil Hume, *Searching for God*, London 1977.

Dom Daniel Rees and others, *Consider Your Call, a Theology of Monastic Life Today,* London 1978.

Dame Maria Boulding, *Marked for Life,* London 1979.